A Solitary Woman

Violet Keppel, before her marriage to Denys Trefusis,
portrait in pastels by M. Ferrini

Henrietta Sharpe

A SOLITARY WOMAN

A life of Violet Trefusis

Constable
London

First published in Great Britain 1981
by Constable and Company Limited
10 Orange Street London WC2H 7EG
Copyright © 1981 by Henrietta Sharpe
ISBN 0 09 464140 4
Set in 11pt Monophoto Ehrhardt by
Servis Filmsetting Limited, Manchester
Printed in Great Britain by
Ebenezer Baylis and Son Limited
The Trinity Press, Worcester and London

For
ENDELLION

A solitary woman! And she went
Singing and gathering flower after flower
With which her way was painted and besprent.

(translated from Dante's *Divine Comedy*
by Percy Bysshe Shelley)

Contents

Acknowledgements

I wish to thank Her Majesty the Queen for her gracious permission to reproduce the photograph of Mr and Mrs Ronald Greville's Whitsun Party.

I thank the following for the evocations and the information they were able to give me about Violet: the Lady Cecilia and Mr David McKenna, Mr Robin McDouall, Miss Naomi Walford, Mr and Mrs John Villiers and family, the Lady Diana Cooper, Miss Lesley Blanch, Mrs John Poë, Mr Timothy Heneage, the Viscount Norwich, the Lord Grimthorpe, Mr Derek Hill, the late Mr Raymond Mortimer, Mr and Mrs James Lees-Milne, Sir Harold Acton, Lady Mosley, Mr Geoffrey Gilmour, M. Gaston Palewski, the Lord William Cavendish-Bentinck, the Bursar Wing Commander Douglas Watson and staff of Charterhouse, the Curator of the Household Cavalry Museum, and lastly Violet's literary executor: Mr John Phillips.

I should particularly like to thank Mr Tim Stranack for being my own personal Patron of the Arts for almost two years, and for the use of his offices and typewriters. For help with the French translation, I am indebted to Mr Jeremy Pilcher and Madame Cole.

And, finally, Lady Cecilia McKenna, Mr Robin McDouall, Mrs John Villiers and Mr Nicholas Hunter Jones were kind enough to read the book in manuscript and gave me much helpful advice and encouragement.

H.F.S.
Primrose Hill, February 1981

Illustrations

[1]

The pride of her parents

Among the profusion of hot-house flowers of the Edwardian era, among the malmaisons and the tuberoses, perhaps the favourite was the violet. Bunches of violets, real or artificial, were pinned to hats, to collars, to bustles. They appeared in the tiny silver vases that cluttered the over-crowded furniture of drawing-rooms; they nestled in huge displays of far prouder blooms in dining-rooms; they emerged rather powdery among the silver-backed brushes, framed photographs and cut-glass scent bottles on dressing-tables. Débutantes wore them on the shoulders of their ball dresses; dowagers fastened them to the collars of their furs; young men sent them in round boxes from smart florists. Violet: the name that evokes an era! Highly fashionable, the name also suggested all things unaffected, unsophisticated, ingenuous, artless and natural. There in one name was acknowledged, instantly and forever, the two sides of the personality of the child who was to be called it.

Violet Keppel was born in Portman Square on 6th June 1894. She came of distinguished antecedents. Her father, the Honourable George Keppel, was the third son of the seventh Earl of Albemarle. Her mother was one of a 'plethora of sisters' born to Sir William and Lady Edmonstone of Duntreath Castle in Stirlingshire.

It is important to stress at once the glamour and charm of Mrs Keppel, both during their zenith at the time of her friendship with Edward VII and afterwards as a great hostess. With her abundant dark hair and turquoise-blue eyes, she was beautiful, but her beauty was less significant than the indefinable quality that drew people to her. People of all ages and from all walks of life who came into contact with her held her in esteem. She was considerate, compassionate and generous, but with no trace of sanctimony; these qualities were impulsive. She had tremendous zest for life, her high spirits were contagious, and she had the gift of making even the most mundane occasion sparkling. Years later, Sir Harold Acton recorded his impression in *More Memoirs of an Aesthete*:

'None could compete with her glamour as a hostess. . . . A fine figure of a woman . . . more handsome than beautiful, she possessed enormous charm, which was not only due to her cleverness and vivacity but to her generous heart. Her kindnesses were innumerable and spontaneous . . . one of the secrets of her success was that she could be amusing without malice; she never repeated a cruel witticism. Above all, she was not snobbish.'

Alice Edmonstone had married the Honourable George Keppel in 1891, to the delight of both families. The young couple, the former from Scotland and the latter from Norfolk, came from similar backgrounds and shared extreme good looks, lack of money being the only cloud in the otherwise clear sky of a perfectly happy marriage. Fitted by the former to move in the highest circles, the young Keppels had moved into a house in Wilton Crescent and taken their place in a society dominated by the Prince of Wales and the Marlborough House set, although the Keppels did not meet the Prince and Princess of Wales until some years later. Queen Victoria still sat on the throne, but since his marriage in 1863, her son had ruled society. Under his aegis, women of the upper and middle classes had acquired a new status. The Prince of Wales thoroughly relished the company of women, particularly those who were attractive and witty, he liked feminine conversation, and enjoyed being consulted on love affairs, on all matters sartorial or pertaining to etiquette. There started to be far fewer lengthy sessions sitting over the claret after dinner. A glass of brandy and a cigar, and then the Prince of Wales was ready to join the ladies. A constant flow of attractive, liberated young ladies from America, as, for example, the Jerome sisters of whom the most beautiful, Jennie, married Lord Randolph Churchill, helped to relax the social atmosphere. Manners gradually became more informal. When Edward first lived at Marlborough House, playing cards and smoking in front of women were both impossible; by the late 1890s, Mrs Keppel was playing bridge with him while she elegantly puffed a cigarette in a long holder.

The elaborate decorations of these ladies' cluttered houses, the emphatically feminine fashions, even the well-ordered daily round, showed just how much women had taken social control. Because they had no entry into politics or business, they put their energies into presiding over the household where they held undisputed sway and where their word was law. Within the home circle, husbands assumed a secondary role. Wives in their turn were expected to behave, and generally did, very much as goddesses, distributing favours and bestowing honours as the whim took them.

Social life centred round delightful women determined to enjoy themselves to the full. A fashionable woman had lovers, but the word did not have the specific sexual meaning it has now, and the exact relationship then was extremely anomalous. Some were simply admirers, from a safe distance, but it was perfectly acceptable for a fashionable married woman to have very close men friends, preferably after she had provided her husband with an heir, and provided the physical aspect were not flaunted. Conventional husbands were expected not to ask too many questions and to accept their wives' lovers, attending the same parties, even country house parties where obliging hostesses ensured that compatible pairs were in conveniently adjacent accommodation. Printed name cards on bedroom doors made the quest of the suppliant admirer less hazardous, as, in some houses, did the ringing of a bell half-an-hour before the house party was officially awoken in order that wanderers could scurry back to their own rooms.

A wife's reputation depended a great deal upon her husband's attitude. If he lent respectability to an affair, the world tended to treat it as respectable. Whatever relations between husband and wife in private, in public he was expected to be polite, attentive and loving.

As they had no identity outside the social round, the cult of worship on the part of men helped to fill the empty hours and the gaps in a woman's existence. Though love affairs could discreetly be consummated, it was the pursuit itself which was important, the endless social round: parties, balls, race meetings, picnics, lun-

cheons, country weekends and visits. All provided further and
different opportunities for the chase, different scenarios for the
same scenes.

Entertaining therefore was immensely important. Luckily everything conspired to make it easy for the hostess.

'Those were wonderful days. Taxation and the cost of living were
low; money was freely spent and wealth was everywhere in
evidence. Moreover it was possessed largely by the nicest people,
who entertained both in London and the country.'[1]*

This was written by someone who knew all about it: man-about-
town George Cornwallis-West, an officer in the Scots Guards and
an expert at all forms of sport, hunting, fishing, shooting and
stalking. He was the son of one of the Prince of Wales' former
favourites, Mrs Patsy Cornwallis-West, and married in 1900 Lady
Randolph Churchill who was some twenty years his senior. In her
book of reminiscences, Lady Randolph describes the time when
beautiful women played such an influential role in society, and the
rise of the Professional Beauties in the 1880s.

'A curious phase had come over society. Publicity became the
fashion. . . . The craze for exhibiting the photographs of "Ladies
of Quality" as they would have been called in the eighteenth
century, was a novelty which brought forth much comment. The
first time mine found its way into a shop, I was severely censured by
my friends, and told I ought to prosecute the photographer.

'So great was the licence allowed to the public that some ladies
who had taken London by storm were publicly mentioned as
"Professional Beauties". Conspicuous among them were Mrs
Langtry and Mrs Wheeler. A fierce war of opinion as to their rival
merits raged about them.'[2]

Other 'P.Bs.' as they soon became known were Lady Helen
Vincent and her sister, the Duchess of Leinster, but the crown was
generally acceded to Georgiana, Lady Dudley.

Although strictly speaking she was a decade too late for the
Professional Beauties, Alice Keppel reigned supreme in a society
still dominated by the ideal of women. At her side, holding her

* Notes and References on p. 190.

umbrella of respectability over her lovely head, was her husband, George. An equally impressive figure physically, he stood well over six foot tall, with broad shoulders, narrow waist and long legs. He had a large aquiline nose, and a magnificent military moustache. He played convincingly his role of obliging husband, and was held in respect and affection. By his wife and daughters, he was much loved and if he inwardly resented his backstage role, he never showed it. It was really a question of facing facts: a young and exquisitely beautiful woman would certainly attract a great many admirers, and if her husband were unable to keep her in the style to which she was entitled, there was probably an eligible sponsor discreetly able to assist those beautiful and well-born ones in the appalling financial burden of keeping up such appearances. In an age when people ate enormously, entertained lavishly, and dressed extravagantly, such a burden could be crippling. George Keppel was in every way unsuited to a business career, even though such a career had begun to be just socially acceptable, and his private income was inadequate.

This realistic approach, tempered with tact and consideration on both sides, made the marriage a great success, a lasting love which endured until the end. Their happiness seemed complete with the arrival of their first child, Violet.

'This Olympian couple first produced a pretty little daughter, curly-headed, dimpled and plump, obviously with looks that dressed up well as early photographs portrayed. This engaging child was a credit at parties and the pride of her parents and nurse. She seemed to cement the beauty of her parents. . . .'[3]

It has often been suggested that Ernest Beckett, later Lord Grimthorpe, was Violet's father, although there is no conclusive evidence for this. Most of her contemporaries believe it to be true, without being entirely sure why.

Ernest William Beckett was born on 25 November 1856, and in October 1883, he married Miss Lucy Lee of New York. He was Member of Parliament for Whitby from 1885 until 1905, when he succeeded his uncle as second Baron Grimthorpe. Apart from his parliamentary duties, he was senior partner in the banking firm of Messrs Beckett & Co., of Leeds. He had three children, Lucy,

Violet as a little girl

Denys dressed
in Russian costume

Helen, and Ralph born in 1884, 1886 and 1891.

It is no secret that on principle Mrs Keppel sensibly liked bankers, and admired people who were clever with money. Ernest Beckett was also a delightful and debonair man of the world. Aged about 35, married for nearly ten years, with a well-established nursery including at last a son and heir, he was possibly at the psychological stage for a love-affair, especially with someone as enchanting as Alice Keppel, in her early twenties, and new to London society. What is not so satisfactorily explained is why she would have wanted such a liaison, unless monetary considerations played a slightly murky part in their dealings. She can only have been married for a year, possibly two, when she met Ernest Beckett, and it was well known, at least within the family circle, that the young Keppels were very much in love. Whatever the truth, however, Violet 'undoubtedly had the Beckett nose' writes Ernest Beckett's grandson,[4] and adds that although there are no records to prove it, he always understood that Alice Keppel was a close friend of his grandfather.

Although later Violet sometimes hinted that Lord Grimthorpe was her real father (he died in 1917), more often she put Edward VII in the role. There is still less evidence for this, even taking into account the fact that Violet began to look distinctly like her (assumed) distinguished antecedents in later life. Like the King, she was to have an uncertain, not to say violent temper, and, when thwarted, was quite capable of hurling the nearest object to hand across the room. Like him too, she had a voracious appetite and, at first anyway, a magnificent digestion. But it is a recorded fact that the King and Mrs Keppel did not meet until February 1898, when Violet was three and a half.

Some people who knew Violet are inclined to believe that Edward VII could have been her father on the grounds that a liaison was carried on in secret for four years before they officially 'met', but it seems entirely unlikely in view of the fact that when they did meet, it was promptly well-known to everyone in society, and neither the King nor Mrs Keppel made any effort to hide the fact that they were close friends. They were seen constantly in each other's company, and indeed it is certainly not in the scope of Mrs

Keppel's honest and straightforward character to hide behind subterfuge. Since Lady Warwick, very young married ladies were more or less out of bounds; Edward confined himself to older ones who could be relied upon to conduct themselves with discretion. Mrs Keppel was now 29, and had been in society long enough to know exactly what the rules were.

The Prince of Wales first caught a glimpse of Alice Keppel when he was inspecting her husband's regiment, the Royal Norfolk Artillery. A few days later, he seized his opportunity to make her acquaintance at Sandown, race-meetings being highly fashionable amusements, where the horses, to some, were of secondary importance. Writing in 1930, George Cornwallis-West recalled the days when admittance to the Royal Enclosure at Ascot cost £2 for the week, and added crushingly, 'In addition, one was able to race more or less in comfort. If one was jostled, it was at least by one's own friends, and not by the curious people that are now met with there.'[5]

No doubt he would still have approved of the order of events in 1898 when the Prince of Wales, crossing the paddock with a friend, encountered the beautiful Mrs Keppel on the arm of an escort, and after introductions had been made, spent the rest of the day with her, apparently immediately and completely captivated.

The world into which Violet was born was a world where nannies, aunts, grandmothers, and especially parents, doted. It was no wonder that this exceptionally pretty little girl soon grew into a spoilt child who resented discipline. Early on, she learned how to use her looks and charm to bend people to her will, and her autobiography, *Don't Look Round*, contains some characteristic strong-willed anecdotes.

Only one voice expressing disapproval had the power to halt Violet in her tracks. Winning her mother's approval was a major incentive to good behaviour. The dreaded, coldly-uttered 'You have no charm' was enough to deter even the most enterprising child. It was not Mrs Keppel's way to raise her voice, or make a scene.

Violet summed up the glamour of her mother in the eyes of a child in her autobiography.

Alice Keppel, Violet's mother, in 1907,
portrait by Flamingue

'I have vivid memories of the first time I accompanied my
mother to the dressmaker where she was received like a goddess,
Monsieur Jean (Worth) supervising her fitting in person, the
vendeuses quite shamelessly forsaking their other clients to vie with
each other in flattering epithets. *Il y avait de quoi*. My mother was
everything that could most appeal to them, lovely, vivacious, fêted,
fashionable, with a kind word for each of the anonymous old crones
who had been for years in the establishment.'[6]

How could any child not be affected by such a mother? With such
an image always before her, it would be difficult not to respond, to
copy, and inevitably, to fail to match up.

Violet's sister, Sonia (born in 1900) has beautifully documented
the early lives led by her sister and herself in *Edwardian Daughter*.
Nursery life was presided over by the powerful figure of Nannie,
whose word was law. In Portman Square, where the Keppels now
lived, a set routine prevailed: day after day the same thing happened
at the same time. Visits to their mother took place twice a day, in the
morning after breakfast, and at tea-time, when the little girls,
befrilled and beribboned, would be fed lumps of sugar soaked in
cream by the various gentlemen being entertained to tea. Enchantingly pretty with her thick dark curls, dressed in white lace-edged
dresses with satin sashes, Violet held the stage. Much encouraged,
she mimicked her mother's friends, the centre of attention. Poor
Sonia, six years younger, and showing no sign of the good looks she
was later to have, was completely overshadowed by her vivacious
elder sister who obviously considered her beneath notice. 'Violet
. . . for the first ten years of my life viewed me with an expression of
unmitigated dislike.'[7]

Out of London, on the round of country house visits which took
place every year, routine was much more relaxed. Cousins and
other children abounded, and games, fishing expeditions and
picnics became the order of the day. Inevitably though there would
be trips downstairs to meet the grown-ups.

On the first of August each year, the Keppels travelled north of
the border to visit various Edmonstone brothers and sisters.
Scotland became, and remained throughout her life, one of Violet's
favourite places.

First they went to Stenton in Perthshire, the home of Uncle Graham, later Viscount Dunedin. 'Architecturally non-committal, the interior was stuffed with all the horrors of the period. A period profaned, enlivened by sport; cluttered up with tennis balls, golf clubs, fishing rods, aquascutums, croquet mallets, waders, gaffs.'[8] Life at Stenton was dominated by the outside, and especially the Tay, the main topic of conversation at meals being that river's moods. Jokes and charades abounded, high spirits were encouraged, and Violet even managed some fishing.

More refined was the atmosphere at Belmont, the house of Aunt Sophie outside Edinburgh. It provided a quiet interlude before the last of the Scottish visits, to romantic Duntreath in Stirlingshire, the home of Uncle Archie, Aunt Ida, and their three sons.

After describing the castle, and especially the strong smell of mince that pervaded it ('I refuse to mince mince'), Violet goes on to say:

'I have completely misled you, if you imagine that Duntreath was a dour Scottish fastness, reeking of Balmorality: it was nothing of the kind. It was romantic, of a standard of luxury without equal in those days; gay, with a touch of Frenchness in its *salons en enfilade*, and premeditated perspectives. One fled from terror to enchantment. The atmosphere of the place was complex, half mediaeval, half exotic. The Greek goddess wedded to the Scottish ogre.'[9]

Until the end of October, day succeeded day, each one filled with shooting, fishing, cricket, games. But Uncle Archie was not like Uncle Graham at Stenton. 'He detested sport, winced through the glorious 12th, took little or no interest in fishing. Gardening was his hobby.'[10] Here Violet, always receptive to atmosphere and beautiful houses, relaxed, and became involved in the local community, walking, exploring and painting.

Holidays at an end, punctually the Keppels returned to London on 1st November, dressing by electricity to catch the early train, a return dreaded by Violet. 'How I used to dread the return to London on November 1st. . . . I have consistently loathed London ever since I can remember, I hated everything about it – streets, climate, smell. As far as I was concerned, there was no redeeming feature.'[11]

Her dread was fairly short-lived, however, for at Christmas, the household would be on the move again, usually to Crichel, the country house of Lord and Lady Alington. Immensely rich, the Alingtons were prominent figures in society, and lived opposite the Keppels in Portman Square. Lord Alington was one of Alice Keppel's staunchest admirers.

Luxury and ostentatious extravagance characterised Christmas at Crichel. Lady Alington ruled that the ladies must all receive jewellery made in semi-precious stones by Fabergé. The guests usually numbered twenty to thirty and the party was arranged for the enjoyment of the adults, children being kept well out of sight except for the statutory visits downstairs each day. Sonia Keppel described Christmas at Crichel: with all its glittering luxury, there was a lack of real warmth and she felt 'like a needle in an enormous work-basket in great danger of being mislaid'.[12]

On Christmas Eve, everyone, including the children, came down to dinner in fancy dress. There exists a ravishing photograph of Violet, aged ten, dressed as a Bacchante, with a bunch of grapes in her hair and a goblet in her hand, standing by a fire-screen at Crichel. Sonia appeared as a minute replica of her great uncle, Admiral Harry Keppel.

More enjoyable, from a child's point of view, was New Year spent, as it usually was, at Melbury Park, home of Lord and Lady Ilchester. If at Crichel, all the fun was arranged for grown-ups, at Melbury it was arranged for the children, usually a dozen or so, and after the magnificent protocol, a more relaxed informality prevailed. Within the large park, the children were free to roam at will, returning only to eat vast meals before dashing out for more games. Coming downstairs was no longer an ordeal. At Melbury, it was house rules for the grown-ups to devise games for the fun of the children, games like 'Pirates', and 'Are You There, Moriarty?'

There were continual visits to other children in the neighbourhood, an endless flow of familiar faces from previous years, more games, more parties, more shrieks of laughter and high-spirited fun.

Back in London after New Year, it was unrelenting nursery routine until the spring holidays, which were spent at Biarritz and

Quidenham, home of Violet's uncle, Lord Albemarle.

After winter in London, Quidenham provided a refuge for Violet, 'an enchantment, carpeted with daffodils, primroses, bluebells, and nests to be found for the searching every hundred yards or so'.[13]

She adored her Aunt Gertie who had the same happy knack as Alice Keppel of bringing out the best in people and making those around her feel content.

Life at Quidenham was not so luxurious as at some of the country houses Violet was used to. A little reminder to Aunt Gertie seemed to be needed.

'"Aunt Gertie, have you no cows?"

'"No cows? Why, you have only to look out of the window!"

'"Well, if you have so many cows, why is there no cream?"'[14]

Uncle Arnold had had a distinguished career as a soldier in the South African war but his talents were many and diverse. He sculpted, painted and built boats, as well as pursuing sporting activities. He could be fierce but his sternness was usually tempered with his sense of humour. Quidenham echoed with laughter, alternating with roars of rage.

There were five cousins: Walter, Arno, Rupert, Betty and Edward. Edward, the youngest, was the bane of Violet's nurse.

'Once his nanny had gone to Norwich, leaving ours supreme. She lisped to him in the garden "Time you came in now!". Edward, aged six, holland pinafore, large straw hat, perennially grazed knees, "I'll trouble you to look after your *own* children, Mrs Eeles, and I'll look after myself!"'[15]

Very different from the relaxed family atmosphere at Quidenham was Easter spent at Biarritz as the guests of Sir Ernest Cassel at the Villa Eugénie. Now intimate friend, royal banker and financial adviser to the King, Sir Ernest had led a fascinating life. Born in Cologne, the son of a Jewish money-lender, he had at sixteen arrived at Liverpool as an immigrant, clutching a violin and a small bag of clothes. He found a job in a grain merchant's office at fifteen shillings a week. By the age of twenty-two, he was earning £5,000 a year in the London firm of Jewish bankers, Bischoffsheim and Goldsmid. From then on, his financial wizardry became legendary, and when he died in 1921, he left over £6 million. Generous

contributions of over £2 million to charities had brought Ernest
Cassel to the notice of King Edward, and the two became close
friends, indeed Sir Ernest's nickname was Windsor Cassel. The
tragedies of his life were the death of his adored wife after only three
years of marriage, and the poor health of their only daughter,
Maud, who died in 1911.

The Villa Eugénie, where Sir Ernest yearly provided accommodation for Mrs Keppel and her daughters during March/April was
vast and ornate. It had been designed for the Empress Eugénie in
1855 by Auguste Déodat Couvrechef, complete with a decorative
watchtower on the cliff. A frequent visitor to the Villa was the King,
staying at the nearby Hôtel du Palais. Both Violet and Sonia had an
informal relationship with this august personage – famous is the
story of the buttered toast sliding down the royal trousers – and he
seemed to enjoy indulging their whims, and spoiling them with
beautiful presents. Perhaps it was the glimpse of their family life he
enjoyed so much. The King was accompanied by his fox terrier,
whose collar bore the inscription 'I am Caesar, the King's dog'.

Sir Ernest's sister acted as hostess at the Villa Eugénie, and in his
party would be his daughter, Mrs Wilfrid Ashley, and her two
daughters, Edwina and Mary. Nobody knew how much it cost Sir
Ernest to make such a generous gesture to his sovereign, but no
doubt he felt himself to be amply rewarded by the continuing good
humour of the King. Even when the weather was bad, Mrs Keppel
contrived to keep the King in a sunny mood.

As neither Queen Alexandra nor George Keppel ever accompanied the party, the King and Mrs Keppel were free to enjoy
themselves uninhibited by the awkwardness which her position in
his life gave rise to in London. There were no embarrassing
problems of protocol here. The local people carefully preserved the
assumed anonymity of the interesting couple, playing up to the
King, pretending not to know who he was, to his great delight.

Grand luxury prevailed. The King's fleet of dark red motor cars
left England a week before he did to make the long journey by road,
so as to be ready for excursions all over the surrounding
countryside. Frequently these excursions included elaborate picnics, often by the side of the road. Since the spots for the picnics

Sir Ernest Cassel,
Alice Keppel's financial adviser and friend of Edward VII
to whom he bore a close physical resemblance

Violet and her younger sister Sonia

were chosen by the King, it is to be assumed that unaccountably he minded neither the crowds that inevitably gathered, nor the dust that settled over the food.

The holiday over, Alice Keppel and her daughters travelled back to England, staying in Paris on the way. To the French, who have always held the great mistresses of powerful kings in proper respect, the beautiful and wise Mrs Keppel epitomised everything a *maîtresse-en-titre* should be. Since she was the darling of the French railway officials as well, these journeys might almost have become royal processions, except for Mrs Keppel's unfailing discretion. Refusing to take advantage of the situation, she resolutely kept to her carriage, not even taking her meals in the dining car.

To Sonia's infant eyes, the metamorphosis that came over her elder sister was one of the more memorable aspects of these trips. 'Violet . . . seemed to galvanise on French soil. From lead she became mercury, laughing and vivacious. I hardly recognised her . . .'[16]

In Paris, the cynosure of London society went straight to Worth to replenish her wardrobe in readiness for the season about to begin. Then they all travelled back to Portman Square, where George Keppel warmly welcomed his wife and daughters.

It is perhaps not surprising that years later some of the heroines in Violet's novels would suffer the same haunting fate as their author, that the influences of their childhoods would always be the strongest elements in their lives, and reality would fail to live up to the expectations raised by such childhoods. Real life could never be anything but second best by comparison.

[2]

A terrible flirt

The first meeting of Violet and Vita Sackville-West took place in 1904 and has been documented by both, Violet thus:

'One day I allowed myself to be dragged to a tea-party at Lady Kilmorey's. There I met a girl older than myself, but, apparently, every bit as unsociable. She was tall for her age, gawky, most unsuitably dressed in what appeared to be her mother's old clothes. I do not remember who made the first step. Anyhow, much to my family's gratification I asked if I might have her to tea. She came. We were both consummate snobs, and talked, chiefly, as far as I can remember, about our ancestors. I essayed a few superior allusions to Paris. She was not impressed; her tastes seemed to lie in another direction. She digressed on her magnificent home in the country, her dogs, her rabbits.

'I thought her nice, but rather childish (I was then ten). We separated, however, with mutual esteem. The repressions of my short life immediately found an outlet in a voluminous correspondence. I bombarded the poor girl with letters which became more exacting as hers tended to become more and more of the "yesterday-my-pet-rabbit-had-six-babies" type. Clearly, no letter writer. Our meetings, however, atoned for this epistolary pusillanimity. These were devoted mainly to the discussion of our favourite heroes – d'Artagnan, Bayard, Raleigh. We used to sit dangling our legs over the leather fender of my father's sitting-room (he was never in at this hour) until fetched by our respective governesses. Our friendship progressed all that winter. I was invited to stay at Knole.'[1]

And by Vita: 'I . . . closed instantaneously in friendship, or almost instantaneously (to be exact, the second time we saw each

other), with Violet. I was thirteen, she was two years younger, but
in every instinct she might have been six years my senior. It seems
to me so significant now that I should remember with such
distinctness my first sight of her; we met at a tea-party by the
bedside of a mutual friend with a broken leg, and she made to me
some little remarks about the flowers in the room. I wasn't listening;
and so didn't answer. This piqued her – she was already spoilt. She
got her mother to ask mine to send me to tea. I went. We sat in a
darkened room, and talked – about our ancestors, of all strange
topics – and in the hall as I left she kissed me. I made up a little song
that evening, "I've got a friend". I remember so well. I sang it in my
bath.'[2]

Two little girls with glamorous dominant mothers, one outgoing,
the other unsociable, they were almost instantly attracted by what
they recognized in the other. They had read the same books and
admired the same heroes. They were both incurably romantic and
saw romance in each other's backgrounds. Vita lived at one of the
largest private houses in England, Knole, near Sevenoaks in Kent, a
sombre house filled with beautiful things. Portraits of dead
Sackvilles gazed down from the walls; there were endless vast
rooms and echoing corridors where they could make up games and
enact dramas. In the Keppels' house in Portman Square, there was
always the excitement that it might be one of the days when the
King was visiting and there was the fun and allure of Mrs Keppel.
Both little girls loved their fathers, but both had 'second fathers'.
Violet had 'Kingy' and Vita 'Seery': Sir John Murray Scott, a
jovial, immensely rich, twenty-five-stone giant. 'I took one as much
for granted as the other', said Vita.[3]

After the second meeting in Portman Square, the two girls
decided they were friends and for the next fourteen years that
friendship endured, though meetings were of necessity fairly
infrequent because both girls travelled abroad extensively. Occasionally these foreign trips would be made in each other's company,
or they would meet in Florence or in Paris, accompanied by
governesses. Endless letters, at least on Violet's part, filled the gaps.

Throughout the years until the spring of 1911, when Violet was
sent to Munich with Sonia, so that the two girls could learn

German, Violet and Vita were to remain close. In 1908, they spent the spring in Florence. Staying at different *pensions*, the two girls spent their days together. Vita was accompanied by an older friend, Rosamund Grosvenor, the daughter of a neighbour in Sevenoaks. Rosamund, with whom Vita subsequently became intimate, was jealous of Violet's influence over Vita and resentful of the feeling of exclusion she experienced when the three went on outings.

Before leaving London, Violet had told Vita that she loved her, and Vita had tried hard to respond to this. That autumn the relationship developed when Vita went to stay with Violet at her Uncle Archie Edmonstone's castle in Stirlingshire. Against the romantic background of the vast Scottish mansion, the passionate natures of the two friends were given full rein. Their imaginations carried them into worlds peopled by their heroes of fiction; they acted scenes from their favourite plays, read aloud to each other, explored secret staircases, and gave each other thrills in pursuit of the castle's home ghosts. Vita recalled the visit twelve years later:

'I remember various details about that visit: how Violet had filled my room with tuberoses, how we dressed up, how she chased me with a dagger down the long passage of that very ancient Scotch castle, and concluded the day by spending the night in my room. It was the first time in my life I ever spent the night with anyone, though goodness knows it was decorous enough: we never went to sleep, but talked throughout the night, while little owls hooted outside. I can't hear owls now without recalling her soft troubling presence in my room in the dark.'[4]

In 1909 and 1910 the paths of the two friends diverged widely. Mrs Keppel wished Violet to acquire complete fluency in French, Italian and Spanish by extensive visits to those countries, in the company of her governess, while Vita, two years older, was now ready to come out. Her new status in the adult world perhaps served to put more than physical distance between her and Violet. Vita was soon caught up in a social whirl of luncheons, dinner parties, balls, country weekends, picnics, race meetings and any other sort of social occasion that could be devised by enterprising Edwardian hostesses, although this, her first season, was greatly overshadowed by the death of the King in May 1910.

Violet and her cousin Rupert at Quidenham Hall

The death of Edward VII had much further reaching effects in
the Keppel household. Sonia Keppel recalled in *Edwardian
Daughter* how life changed completely afterwards. The family
moved straight out of the house in Portman Square so as to escape
condolences, and went to stay with Mr and Mrs Arthur James in
Grafton Street. For the first time, Mrs Keppel seemed stern and
unsmiling; when the two girls went to visit her in her bedroom, 'She
turned and looked at us blankly and without recognition, and rather
resentfully, as though we were unwelcome intruders'.[5]

Whatever worries and heartbreaks were caused by the King's
death, financial worries had long since been dismissed. Mrs
Keppel, expertly advised by Sir Ernest Cassel, was a rich woman.
(In 1919, Violet could write to Vita, 'Chinday (their secret name for
Mrs Keppel) has at least £20,000 a year'.) Their new London house
was to be number 16 Grosvenor Street, an imposing house
exquisitely decorated and arranged by a connoisseur of beauty,
although it was not ready for them to move into for two years. A
house magnificently suited to entertaining, seventy guests could be
seated at once in the dining room.

With the famous tact which unfailingly led her to steer the right
course between the twin rocks of what was acceptable and what was
not, Mrs Keppel retired from society overnight. Visits from friends
in the country took up the summer and in November, the whole
family left for Ceylon. It was not until the season of 1912 that Alice
Keppel took her place in society again, by which time any
awkwardness arising from her position had been smoothed by the
passage of time.

According to Violet, she and her sister were given just four days
to prepare for the trip to Ceylon. To Violet, leaving London at any
time was a good idea, and leaving a London smothered in
November fog seemed like the realisation of a dream. Her
imagination reeled.

'A procession of visionary elephants poured into the school-room
with young, turbaned rajahs culled from Dulac on their backs.
Cobras undulated, macaws screeched, sepoys salaamed.'[6]

Sir Thomas Lipton had lent the party his bungalow at
Dambatenne, set amid tea plantations 6,000 feet above sea level.

Mr and Mrs Ronald Greville's Whitsun Party, Reigate, 1905. Among the guests was Edward VII. Alice Keppel is seated second from right

They stayed three months. Precocious, inspired letters to Vita poured from Violet's pen, always in her impeccable French:

   '*Sous un ciel flamboyant de midi tropical la route de Maradene poudroie. . . . de chaque côté s'élèvent des imprévus arbres au feuillage tour à tour sombre, chatoyant, ou lustré. La chaleur est telle que le moindre geste est une corvée . . . Plus loin dans un tourbillon de poussière, on aperçoit de grands boeufs las, à l'oeil injecté de sang, à l'échine balafrée d'horions. A côté, noirs, luisants, fourbus, les bouviers.*

   '*Partout du reflet, partout de la lumière – et puis, de temps à autre, une noix de coco qui se détache, lentement, avec un bruit mat, sur la terre brune. Une terre de tout repos, une terre de toute beauté, une terre pleine, une terre inouï, exhalant tous les fruits, toutes les épices – les candeurs d'une terre vermeille éprise de la lumière, ivre de soleil. . . .*'[7]

(Beneath the blazing sky of a tropical noon, the road to Maradene crumbles to powder . . . on each side arise unexpected trees: their foliage by turns sombre, shimmering or glossy. The heat is such that the slightest movement is an effort. Further off, in a whirlwind of dust, great weary oxen may be seen with their blood-shot eyes and their backs scarred by blows. To one side stand the herdsmen burnished black and gleaming.

   Reflections and light everywhere, and then, now and again a coconut would slowly fall with a dull sound on to the brown earth. A country of absolute repose and of absolute beauty, a rich and unbelievable one, redolent with every fruit and every spice – the artlessness of a vermilion earth in love with light, and drunk with sunshine.)

   Even from that distance and from those exotic distractions, Violet sensed that Vita had grown away from her. Pathetic, she sought reassurance:

   'One looks in vain for some coherence, some tell-tale blade of grass in the inextricable labyrinth which is your last letter – a labyrinth, alas, which lacks an Ariadne to provide the guiding thread.

   'But after a brief attempt, I give up guessing! It's too hot to slave away at it. Unless you have suddenly fallen in love with some happy mortal, I confess myself incapable of reading between the lines. Oh well, this will sort itself out.

'As I carefully read it again, a sort of dull anguish which I can only describe as apprehension makes my heart suddenly beat more rapidly and my hand tremble as I write. . . .

'It's both thrilling and sad.

'For the first time your extra two years seem very real to me, overbearing and ominous.

'But don't think that I hadn't foreseen this moment: I have often dwelt on it.

'Oh for goodness' sake, tell me that I am wrong, that it is my reckless imagination which is leading me astray.

'After all, I'm only a woman. I ought to have foreseen that perhaps at your age a liaison with a man would happen. I would do well to leave it at that. I feel that I'm about to say things best left unsaid. You won't laugh, promise me that you won't laugh. It's a long time since I've asked anything of you, so grant me this. It would hurt so . . .'.[8]*

In other letters, she attacked, deploring the lack of letters from Vita, insufficient depth of feeling when they did come, and their writer's preoccupation with being a social success. For Vita was a success, and whatever her reservations, she enjoyed grand parties and they occupied a great deal of her time.

The visit to Ceylon ended in the spring of 1911. George and Alice Keppel continued to travel east, to China. The two girls, accompanied by their nanny and governess, went to learn German, in Munich, 'dumped down, like the Babes in the Wood, in an exclusively German forest'.[9] At nearly seventeen, Violet was already fluent in French and Italian, and spoke good Spanish.

The separation from their parents, and the prospect of isolation together in a new and friendless land precipitated at last the first tentative moves of friendship between the sisters. According to Sonia, the first words Violet ever addressed directly to her were spoken as the Keppels left their daughters on the first stage of their

* The original French of this and following quotations is given in the Notes and References.

journey to Germany. 'Violet and I watched Mamma together. And, from that moment, for me, the 8,000 mile long voyage to Ceylon was justified. As we went below to our cabins, Violet bade me "good night".'[10]

En route to Munich, Violet stayed for two nights at Monte Carlo where Lady Sackville, alarmed that Vita might be consumptive after an attack of pneumonia in the summer of 1910, had rented a villa, the Château Malet. Harold Nicolson, a young man who worked at the Foreign Office and to whom Vita had become rather attached during her first season, had also been to stay, and his visit had left Vita half-disappointed, half-relieved that he treated her only as a friend. She found his companionship delightful.

Another visitor was Rosamund Grosvenor, invited by Lady Sackville. 'I would never have dreamt of asking anyone to stay with me; even Violet had never spent more than a week at Knole.'[11] Vita went on to record how, although she had been unwelcome at first, her feelings for Rosamund had developed, so that, 'By the middle of that summer (1911) we were inseparable, and moreover were living on terms of the greatest possible intimacy. . . . I was very much in love with Rosamund'.[12] Unfortunately Rosamund's attraction for her was almost exclusively physical. Vita found her stupid. She had a cloyingly sentimental nature and the contrast with Harold was immediately apparent to her. But at this stage she thought of Harold in terms of great friendship only.

In the Wagnerian fastness of Munich, Violet was meanwhile learning German with her usual linguistic facility, and acquiring some peculiar friends at the *pension* where they were staying and at school. Her friendship with Sonia had grown apace too, despite the fact that Violet had developed a strange taste for practical jokes. 'At long last, having achieved her friendship, I was not going to dispute the terms of it. Especially as now, she was proving herself immensely funny after her decade of silence', wrote Sonia years later in *Edwardian Daughter*. Then Mrs Keppel arrived, not amused.

'There was no disguising her . . . dismay at the metamorphosis wrought by Germany on her elder daughter. She had left a fairly presentable young girl, unobtrusively dressed in Woollands' coats and skirts; now a budding Gretchen met her gaze, fatuous, shapeless, wearing a silver watch-chain round her middle with a silver watch worn in guise of a sporran. She took one look at me: "My poor child!" she exclaimed. "You can never leave Germany!"

'I was much hurt.

'"Why, Mama? Surely you wanted me to learn German and to like Germany?"

'For the first time she was up against my fatal adaptability.

'"Yes, darling, I know, I wanted you to learn German, but I never thought you would *turn into* a German. After all, I thought you had completely identified yourself with France; you can't be *both* German *and* French."

'"Oh, yes, I can, one can like Sandkuchen and – and *mille feuilles*!"

'"That's exactly what you are, a *mille feuilles*; well, there's a *feuille* too many. It's time I took you both away . . ."'[13]

Despite this, the girls stayed another six months, no longer at the uncomfortable Pension Glocker but in a sunny flat further up the same street. Typically, Mrs Keppel had arranged everything to suit everyone. She found them some suitable friends, and life suddenly became fun, given up to painting, ski-ing and music. Violet wrote a play in German and invited her new friends to take part. George Keppel arrived and took his completely moonstruck elder daughter to the opera. Hand in hand, they sat entranced through a performance of *Tristan*. Vita and London seemed another world away.

Vita had left Monte Carlo in April 1911 and returned home for the season. At the end of that summer, Harold Nicolson returned from Madrid and they began to meet again at parties. Although he had been very much in her thoughts, Vita was deeply involved with Rosamund Grosvenor. She was, however, delighted to see him and as he began to spend more and more time sitting in her pocket, and people began to tell her that he was in love, she started wanting to believe that it was true. She preferred him to all the other young men she had met, and she had many admirers, including Lord Lascelles

A shooting party at Quidenham Hall. Edward VII is seated on the left. George Keppel stands on the extreme right.

(who married Princess Mary in 1922) and Lord Granby. Harold had nothing like Harewood or Belvoir behind him, although he came from an excellent diplomatic family and had himself succeeded in winning a much-coveted position in the Foreign Office. By Christmas, Vita was hoping that he would propose.

She could not think of Harold in terms of physical love; that side of her nature was completely absorbed by Rosamund. At this stage, Vita only vaguely realised her dual nature. She thought she could not be in love physically with Harold because of Rosamund. Rosamund was possibly only a passing fancy to her and once she had been forgotten, Vita would be able to become the perfect wife and mother. This in effect was how she tried to rationalise her life, and for a short time it seemed to work. She did not reckon with the explosive force that was Violet. For Violet was no second Rosamund.

The New Year began with a round of country house dances. Vita was sure that Harold meant to propose to her at a ball at Hatfield House and, with characteristic single-mindedness, set her heart on going, even though Seery had died on 17th January. There was no parental opposition to her going to Hatfield and Harold did propose. Vita accepted, but the Sackvilles would not permit a public announcement of the engagement as they thought Vita and Harold too young to be sure of their feelings and there was the question of settlements. Harold was on the point of leaving for Constantinople, and they were told they might write to each other as 'ordinary friends'. After Harold left, Vita took to her bed, depressed at the anti-climax. As she improved, Rosamund began to fill her life again, and in the spring of 1912, they went together to Florence, accompanied by a governess. Sharing a three-roomed cottage, they were able to give full expression to their feelings for each other. Harold was still a beautiful idea, the ideal husband. She could not imagine him in terms of bed.

Harold returned to England in August and he and Vita spent much of the time at Knole, their love for each other growing. One evening, Harold kissed Vita for the first time and after that they made a fuss about the vague terms of their engagement, insisting that they might write to each other as fiancés, instead of just friends.

This was agreed. In October, Harold left for Constantinople, accompanied by Vita and Rosamund as far as Bologna, where they left him to go to Florence.

It was here, during October and November, that Vita's affair with Rosamund reached its height. Extraordinary as it may seem, secure in her love for Harold, she confessed herself 'never so much in love with Rosamund as during those weeks in Italy and the months that followed'.[14] In an effort to rationalise the two loves, one bright in its unsullied purity, the other inverted, Vita sought for an explanation. She could only account for it to herself by putting each love into a separate compartment. That for Harold was separate, apart, untouched by baser 'perverted' feelings for those such as Rosamund. This was her moral code, which lasted all her life, except when the landslide that was Violet threatened to engulf her.

Still desperately trying to reconcile her heart and her feelings, Vita went to Spain. In May, she suddenly lost confidence in her feelings for Harold, but a forceful telegram from him restored her faith, and on 5th August 1913, their engagement was announced. They were married in the chapel at Knole on the 1st October, and departed for Constantinople, honeymooning en route.

Meanwhile, back in Munich there was Violet, a rather plump seventeen-year-old, with well-developed musical and literary tendencies, and four languages to her credit, in various stages of fluency.

From Munich to Paris: Violet longed to make her *début* in Paris, but Mrs Keppel was adamant. Paris was only to prepare Violet for London.

'After a month in Paris, who would have recognised the Bavarian Backfish? Patiently, tirelessly, my mother dealt with my appearance, item after item; complexion, hair, figure, clothes, adding here, subtracting there. A whole *quartier* concentrated on my uninviting person'.[15]

Thus streamlined, remodelled, fashionably chic, Violet returned to Grosvenor Street and her coming-out ball. Violet recounted in *Don't Look Round* how she was immediately labelled as a blue-stocking, and in the younger set nothing could have been more fatal to her chances of success. To make up for it, she became a flirt, and was immediately designated as 'fast' – fatal with mamas. Moving in the circles that she did, there was no shortage of eligible invitations for Mrs Keppel's daughter, but Mrs Keppel's daughter did not always conform.

All her life, Violet hated huge impersonal parties, unless she were the centre of attention. She much preferred intimate gatherings, such as small dinner parties where she could display her brilliant conversational skill. At large parties, she tended to isolate herself with one person, sitting close to him or her on the sofa, deep in conversation.

Imperceptibly at first, the foundations of her hitherto marvellously secure and happy life began to shift. Until now she had been a child, a spoilt child, most of whose whims had been instantly gratified by indulgent adults. Everything had worked for her. Constant travelling had brought her the intellectual stimulus she needed; there had been a continuous stream of new impressions to keep her interested. Now Violet was entering a new phase of her life, where she was responsible for what happened, where she stood alone on her own merits.

How difficult it was to be the daughter of such a mother. Impossible both to compete and not to compete; comparisons were bound to be drawn. If one could not be so beautiful, so universally beloved as one's mother, one could at least be different. Flirting outrageously and perfecting her gift for mimicry soon made Violet a name for herself.

Sonia Keppel, still a schoolgirl, watched her sister's reaction uneasily. It seemed to her that nearly every day there were guests in the big dining room.

'When Violet was not entertaining her friends at home, she was being entertained. And, strangely enough, I do not believe that she much enjoyed either process.'[16]

To Sonia, Violet did not seem happy, did not seem to be enjoying the wonderful season arranged for her by Mrs Keppel. Violet did not seem happy to Lady Diana Manners (later Cooper) either. Somehow she did not fit in; there was to Lady Diana something withdrawn and secretive about Violet, an impression heightened by

her very low-pitched voice (her '*voix clandestine*' as her mother
described it) which meant that anyone conversing with her had to
be very close in order to hear what she was saying.

At the top of the house in Grosvenor Street, Violet had her own
studio 'decorated in the most ridiculous and pretentious Italianate
style, chasubles on the wall, and an ikon over the radiator'.[17] Gold
lamé curtains kept out the light and incense burned exotically
whenever Violet was in residence. Fellow devotees of the Russian
ballet, then very much in vogue, gathered at the studio.

Osbert Sitwell wrote a charming memoir of Mrs Keppel and her
household in 1913 in his book, *Great Morning*:

'I liked greatly to listen to her talking; if it were possible to lure
her away from the bridge-table, she would remove from her mouth
for a moment the cigarette which she would be smoking with an air
of determination, through a long holder, and turn upon the person
to whom she was speaking her large, humorous, kindly, peculiarly
discerning eyes. Her conversation was lit by humour, insight and
the utmost good nature: a rare and valuable attribute in one who
had never had – or, at any rate, never felt – much patience with
fools. Moreover, a vein of fantasy, a power of enhancement would
often lift what she was saying, and served to emphasise the
exactness of most of her opinions, and her frankness. Her talk had
about it a boldness, an absence of all pettiness, that helped to make
her a memorable figure in the fashionable world. The company of
her two daughters added to the pleasure of frequenting her house.
Violet, cosmopolitan and exotic from her earliest years, with a vivid
intelligence, a quick eye for character, which had bestowed on her
an irresistible gift of mimicry and the ability to gather unexpected
pieces of information about people and things which she was wont
to impart in a voice, eager but pitched in so low a tone as sometimes
to be inaudible. . . .'

In the summers of 1913 and 1914, the Keppels stayed at a
country house called Clingendaal near The Hague. Streams of
pretty girls and eligible young men were invited to stay. There was
an endless house party of bright young people: the wonderfully
beautiful Lady Diana Manners, Raymond Asquith, Patrick Shaw
Stewart, Vi de Trafford.

With his immense flair for organisation, George Keppel arranged expeditions down to the last detail: bathing at nearby Scheveningen, visits to the cheese-making towns of Gouda and Alkmaar, picture galleries in The Hague, race-meetings, picnics, sight-seeing. Every meal was a banquet, every evening a party. Surrounded by all this, Violet was still unsettled. Whatever she was looking for in life, it was not to be found in the glittering social round.

'She would come, at first silent, unobtrusive, almost sulky; then . . . by a word or a glance they would be linked, the whole system of their relationship developing itself anew, a system elaborated by her . . .; built up of personal, whimsical jokes; stimulating, inventive, she had to a supreme extent the gift of creating such a web, subtly, by meaning more than she said and saying less than she meant; giving infinite promise, but ever postponing fulfilment.'[18]

The intervening years had changed nothing. To Vita, Violet was 'still a little mad, but charming'. Violet, invited to spend the weekend at Knole, discovered that Vita had grown into a beauty, surrounded by admirers. She retaliated by showing that she too was attractive to men. Bombarding the chosen one with charm, she was whisked off to see the park by moonlight. Visiting Vita in her room later that night, she found Vita unimpressed. Vita wrote in her diary, 'Once she came into my room in the middle of the night and asked me if I were in love; but that was some time before, and I could say No quite truthfully. She always came like that when she had a chance, and she usually kissed me then – on my mouth, I mean – but we never did, even ordinarily at other times. Violet was very amusing then and a terrible flirt, throwing over first one man and then another; she used to do all kinds of parlour-tricks, which I never saw, as she stopped immediately I came into the room, and if we ever met accidentally she would turn white to the lips. I used to amuse myself by taking her unaware in this way, and Dada in the innocence of his heart used to say, "Did she turn pale?" as a joke.'[19]

It was not only Lord Sackville who was innocent. They all were, then.

Violet was still trying to conform. She had flirtations. There was Julian Grenfell, a real feather in her cap as he was well-known to be anti-social. Julian was, like Violet, an individualist, and he was in revolt against society. In common with Violet, he had a beautiful and dominating mother, Lady Desborough. More and more he was finding it difficult to accept her ideals. 'He saw Society around him based on ideals of competitiveness and self-sacrifice; that these were contradictory, and led to fantasy and disaster.'[20]

Violet described her brief interlude with Julian Grenfell in *Don't Look Round*:

'Julian alternately fascinated and terrified me. On one occasion, I dragged him to a ball given by one of my relatives. Bursting out of hired "tails", he lured me to the ladies' cloakroom, where he locked us in. An awkward moment arose when a member of the Royal Family asked for her cloak. Had he been less precipitate he would doubtless have won my consent to – anything.

'Alas! His courtship was too spectacular, the ladies' cloakroom incident did not pass unnoticed. My father was infuriated by his dress, his recurrent black eye, *sans gêne*. Julian was banned.'

The Keppels probably approved more of a friendship with a rich and eligible young diplomat, Lord Gerald Wellesley. In 1913 there was an unofficial engagement before Lord Gerald returned to Constantinople. What happened subsequently is unclear, but the understanding between Violet and Lord Gerald obviously came to an end. He later became the seventh duke, something to which Violet would occasionally refer in later life: 'Of course I could have been the Duchess of Wellington!'

Lady Cynthia Asquith noted in her diary in September 1915 a flirtation with her brother-in-law, Cyril.

'Saturday 11th September

'Beb [her husband, Herbert Asquith] and I dined with the Asquiths. I sat between the P.M. and Mr Meiklejohn . . . Violet Keppel was there and did some brilliant imitations: she has considerable "pig-charm". There is an "affair" between her and Cis, and Beb and I felt sadly *de trop* as everyone else played bridge and we were left alone with them.'[21]

There was a joke announcement of an 'engagement' to Osbert

Julian Grenfell, drawing by Marjorie Manners

Sitwell who had long been a devoted admirer of her mother. There
were few women Osbert Sitwell really liked, and Violet was not
really his type. They shared a love of beautiful things, however, of
Edwardians and Mrs Keppel, of Florence, and their paths crossed
throughout their lives.

With all her young men, Violet was at pains to show the world
that she was attractive to men. Flaunting her love affairs so openly
betrayed her sense of insecurity. She herself was unconvinced of
their value.

At the outbreak of war, the Keppels were at Clingendaal, and
immediately hurried back to London. George Keppel rejoined his
regiment, and Mrs Keppel went to work in a field hospital in
France. Violet, with her sister, went to stay with Lady Ilchester at
Melbury, where they had often stayed as children. For Sonia it was
blissful to be back; the harsh realities of war scarcely touched her.
But Violet became even more unsettled. Deprived of the calming
influence of her mother, and the distractions of her own set in
London, the independence of her studio in Grosvenor Street, she
felt completely lost. There was no one of her particular age group,
or anyone who particularly shared her interests at Melbury, apart
from an aged French governess on whom she could practise her
French. As a distraction this soon palled. There was too much time
to brood, everyone was too busy with their own concerns to be very
sympathetic, and above all, there was the heartbreak of losing so
many friends. Julian Grenfell was one of the first to go, in May
1915.

'When I heard of his death, I refused to believe that anyone so
vital, so gifted, so superb, should have to meet with the common
fate. But I was soon to learn that the *élite* were Death's
favourites.'[22]

Vita, back from Constantinople and in Kent, was no help; she
seemed another person now, immersed in country pursuits and in
maternity. Ben was born in August 1914 and Nigel in January 1917.
The Nicolsons bought their first house, Long Barn, in 1915 and
there began one of the most enduring passions of Vita's life: for
gardens.

Violet, at her own request, was Ben's godmother. She took very

Vita Sackville-West, photographed by Hoppé, June 1916

Knole, Vita Sackville-West's family home

little interest in the child. Vita recalled those days thus:
'There are so few events in those years, except war events. In our
personal life there was nothing except moving to London for the
winter, and to the cottage for the summer, watching Ben grow and
learn to speak, and for me, writing. I should think it was hardly
possible for two people to be more completely and unquestionably
happy. There was never a cloud, never a squabble. I knew that if
Harold died, I should die too; it all made life very simple. I saw
Violet from time to time, but she was more alien from me than
she had ever been, and yet in a way our friendship was on easier
terms, that strange undercurrent had never made itself so little
felt.

'She is very proud and a first-class dissimulator.'[23]

In 1915, Violet and Sonia moved back to Grosvenor Street.
When the Zeppelin raids started, Mrs Keppel insisted on their
sleeping in the drawing room on camp beds, an arrangement which
suited neither and was made worse by the fact that Nannie insisted
on merino combinations being worn under nightdresses in case of
emergency. Violet spent the hours of bombing lying full length
under the dining room table, wearing a tight seal-skin coat and
characteristically sniffing a gardenia.

Later she started work in a canteen for soldiers in Grosvenor
Gardens, an episode which ended with her being sacked for making
a cup of cocoa for a visiting general out of knife cleaning powder.
She would have liked to join Mrs Keppel nursing in France, but it
was generally felt that she might not be very useful.

Her fundamental insecurity intensified by the times, Violet was
still falling in and out of love. There was Bim Tennant, and others,
with whom she formed temporary attachments. None of them
lasted. The novelty wore off. But, in 1918, a new man appeared and
Violet's interest was immediately aroused.

Denys Trefusis was then 28, a handsome officer in the Royal
Horse Guards. He had reddish gold hair and startling blue eyes.
Born in Bickmaster in Somerset on 30th March 1890, he was the
youngest of the four children of the Honourable John Schomberg
Trefusis, who was the fourth son of the nineteenth Lord Clinton.
The baronetcy of Clinton (motto: *Tout vient de Dieu*) had been

40 *A Solitary Woman*

created in 1299 but it was not until the time of the seventeenth baron in the late eighteenth century that the family name became Trefusis. Denys' mother, Eva Louisa, had been born a Bontein and was related to the Graham clan. Through her mother, she claimed descendancy from Shelley. But little poetry or romance dwelt in her soul; like her husband, she was highly respectable and down-to-earth and, if her views on life were inclined to be narrow, they were stamped with the seal of common sense. She was universally known as Mitty because she had adopted a young Scottish boy called Sutherland Dambrech who had a dreadful stammer, the result of trying to make him right-handed when he was naturally left-handed. The child would try to say 'Mrs Trefusis', but it invariably came out as 'Mitty Fusis', and Mitty she remained.

At the time Denys was born, the Trefusis family lived at Thorncombe House, Crowcombe. Colonel Trefusis was the local Master of Foxhounds. In 1897 they moved to Rockbeare, just outside Exeter, from where Denys was sent to Charterhouse at the beginning of the Oration Quarter (Christmas term) in 1903. He was put into Girdlestoneites, named after its somewhat formidable housemaster, Frederick Girdlestone (1844–1922). He was a Carthusian himself, who had been Captain of the School, and after Oxford and the successful beginnings of a career at the Bar, had returned to the school, becoming a housemaster in 1874. He combined his duties at Charterhouse with being a Justice of the Peace in Godalming and twice being its mayor.

The October 1903 issue of *The Carthusian* contained a great deal of useful information about the current state of the school and forthcoming events for that term. It announced that: 'The authorities have at last seen their way to enlarging the much-abused League Grounds on the Promontory. What a boon this is, only those who have played on those grounds can realise'. . . . Some offending trees had been removed, likewise some memorial brasses from the ante-chapel to the new Cloister – 'undoubtedly their proper place'. But there was still overcrowding of the pews in the chapel: 'We are still crowded nine into a row . . . very unhealthy as well as unpleasant'. There had been a decision to start an Old Carthusian Corner in the Magazine and old boys 'who consider their experiences sufficiently interesting' were invited to contribute.

That term there were two debates, the motions before the House being 'That the belief in supernatural appearances is perfectly justifiable' and 'That the English press of today has a demoralizing influence on the people'.

Boys were entertained by the band of the Second Battalion Royal Scots Fusiliers. Another Saturday, Mr Harrison Hill gave 'a delightful entertainment which did not grow at all stale, a fault which is very prone to occur on similar occasions'.

On 10th October, Mr A. Capper, the thought-reader, came and demonstrated knot-tying. He then inveigled three boys into divulging their love affairs.

The Aldershot Staff gave an Assault-at-Arms with displays on the parallel bars, foil fencing, boxing, bayonet-v-bayonet, lance exercise, blindfold boxing and horizontal bar exercises. This was probably the entertainment that appealed most to the young Denys, who was interested in all things military and had, on arrival at the school, been immediately placed in the Rifle Corps, which implied he was a good shot. But his school career was undistinguished: early academic promise proved false, mainly because of a disastrous but rather endearing unwillingness to do any work at all. In the School Monitors' Register, the name of D.R. Trefusis figured prominently: 'Without books', 'Grammar not learnt', 'Idle', 'Grammar neglected', 'Gross inattention'. During his first term alone, his name appeared thirteen times and his ability to quote from the classics must have been impressive by the end of his school career – he had learnt by heart literally thousands of lines of Euripides, Ovid and Virgil!

The high spot of Denys' school career seems to have been on 17th March 1906 when, in 'delightfully fine weather', Charterhouse suffered a crushing defeat by 46 points at the hands of Wellington in a shooting match. Private D.R. Trefusis achieved the second highest score of the day, with 24 points.

But although he did not appear to work at school, he was obviously highly intelligent, for in 1909, when he was 19, he wrote and had published at his own expense *A Short Essay upon Moral*

Retrogression under Socialism – a piece of work that dealt with the disastrous effects that socialism would have on the world he knew. While deploring the extreme poverty in which some sections of society were forced to live, and the curse of unemployment, he pointed out how little socialism would do to improve the lot of such people, and systematically showed what would be the effects of socialism on liberty, patriotism, morality and religion.

> It seems to me that Socialism must abandon all Hope, both for this world and hereafter. There is to be no reward for hours of daily toil, and there is to be no reward for the long labour of life. I cannot see why man should care to live without hope; life would be too dismal to keep his spirit alive, and his body had better die with it.

It is the work of an idealist – a young man who, having just left school, has been brought up patriotically to respect the Church, the Army and above all family life, particularly the part played by women. His view is reassuringly Edwardian:

> And what will become of women under this code? Socialism avowedly aims at the emancipation of woman and the equality of the sexes. Yet the practical effect of this new code of morality will be that woman, owing to physical inferiority – and that she can never overcome – will become almost entirely the slave of man, and an accomplice to his immorality. She will be lowered at once to the status of the women of an Eastern harem. Is this to be the fate of woman, to whom we men owe so much in the happiness of our lives, for whom we profess so much respect, whose purity we have always held as one of the most beautiful and the most lovable things in all creation?

Colonel Trefusis, possibly at a slight loss when faced by this closely argued composition, sent copies to his friends, whose reactions were flattering. The Revd H.E. Hyde, Vicar of Bovey Tracey, wrote on 22nd February 1910, '. . . since the writer has been able to produce so creditable a piece written so simply and intelligibly at 19, you may look forward with confidence to some admirable literary work from him as the years go by'.

Denys Trefusis as an officer in the Household Cavalry

Soon after the publication of his essay, Denys had gone to Russia, where he became tutor to the children of an aristocratic family who owned a large *dacha*. This was the beginning of his love for Russia, and when he learnt to speak the language with such masterly fluency. He stayed in Russia until September 1914, when he returned to England and joined the Royal Horse Guards as a second lieutenant.

In later years, Violet would say that Denys had run away to Russia from school but this was probably one of her romantic myths about him. And she had several, the first being his appearance.

He had a pale, arrogant face, whose logical conclusion would seem to be a pointed beard; I mentally added a ruff and one pearl ear-ring. It was impossible to look better bred, more audacious. Slim and elegant, he could not help dramatising his appearance . . . he made the most ordinary clothes appear picturesque.[24]

It was not just the way he looked that attracted her, however; to Violet he had a special quality which she described as his Slav charm. Later on, in her first novel, *Sortie de secours*, her heroine succumbs to exactly the same sort of bewitchment, and it is defined thus:

'Slav charm – by which I mean that mixture of brutality and caress, that taste for the embroidered truth, that foresight into the unforeseeable, those childish excesses and those outrages.'[25]

But perhaps the most appealing facet of Denys Trefusis was the fact that it was not going to be easy to get him to fall in love with her. He had the same elusive quality that had drawn her towards Julian Grenfell and, like Julian Grenfell, he had the attraction of the unattainable. Violet embarked on her special technique. She bombarded him out in the trenches with her clever, witty letters.

Denys had spent the whole of the war in France and Flanders with the British Expeditionary Force, and apart from two months in England in 1915 when he had influenza, he had not been invalided home. This was surprising in view of the fact that he had a habit of walking up and down the parapet, an easy mark for enemy gunfire which frequently flashed but never hit. This dare-devil attitude endeared him to his men for whom it provided a distraction from the loathsome monotony of knee-deep rat-infested mud, and the consequent horrors of trench-foot. But recklessness suggests doubt – that Denys was wondering, as so many of his generation were, what the vileness and hell were all for. He seemed to be searching for some kind of motivation. In such confusion, Violet's letters hit their target. Denys began to respond.

Eventually he proposed marriage, but by then it was too late. Something much more heart-shattering had to run its course.

[3]
A lark with clipped wings

As the war drew to its close in 1918, Violet invited herself to Long Barn to stay, ostensibly because she was frightened by the threat of bombs in London. Vita was bored by the idea, worried Violet would be both bored and boring. At first, it seemed as if her fears were justified. Violet went up to London during the day, returning to the peace and quiet of Kent only for the night. Then on 18th April, everything changed.

That particular day, Violet did not go up to London for the day, and Harold Nicolson did not return from London for the night. Vita recounts in her diary how all that day she had been wildly exhilarated, leaping over fences in her newly-acquired breeches while Violet trailed behind her, strangely submissive. That evening, after dinner, the barriers in Vita suddenly went down and for four hours she talked, talked herself hoarse, while Violet, in rose-red velvet, lay on the sofa, quite silent. As Vita poured her heart out in a sudden urgent self-realisation of her dual personality, Violet lay and listened. When Vita had finished, Violet took up the threads and spun them into dreams. With infinite subtlety, she directed them towards the special and secret feeling that had always existed between them, made it seem inevitable and predestined. Taking Vita's hands, she counted the ways she loved Vita. In her low husky voice, she struck chords which awoke responses in Vita. So beautifully was this done that Vita was completely enslaved, yet liberated. Enslaved by this new vision of Violet, she was at last liberated from the need to conform, the need to suppress her true self exclusively in marital love, and dutiful maternity. Dazzling vistas of unbounded freedom rolled out before her. She would become a great writer, devoting her life to beauty, unfettered by convention. In the foreground lay Violet, not brash and noisy, nor playing the fool, but humble, serious, and perfectly in tune with Vita's mood. In her crimson dress, with her shadowy great grey eyes and red mouth, in her new mood of sweet seriousness, she seemed to epitomise femininity. To Vita, she was infinitely seductive.

'A cloak of black velvet . . . a dusky voice, a gipsy among voices! the purple ripeness of a plum; the curve of a southern cheek; the heart of red wine. All things seductive and insinuating. It matched her soft indolence, her exquisite subtlety, her slow, ironical smile.'[1]

Two kisses were exchanged. Vita did not sleep all night.

This then was the beginning. There was to be no going back.

Violet lit in Vita a flame that was soon to become a raging fire, threatening to ravage everything in its path. Emotionally, spiritually, and physically, they were united.

'What was it, this bond of flesh? So material, yet so imperative, so compelling, as to become almost a spiritual, not a bodily necessity? So transitory, yet so recurrent? dying down like a flame, to revive again? so unimportant, so grossly commonplace, yet creating so close and tremulous an intimacy? this magic that drew together their hands like fluttering butterflies in the hours of sunlight, and linked them in the abandonment of mastery and surrender in the hours of night? that swept aside the careful training, individual and hereditary, replacing pride by another pride?'[2]

After the fateful evening of 18th April, Vita and Violet's first impulse was to go away together, and they were lent a cottage at Polperro by Hugh Walpole, whom Violet had known since he had been tutor to her cousins at Duntreath. The fortnight in Cornwall was a blissful interlude which only strengthened the feelings that had flared between them in Kent. On her return, Vita began to write *Challenge*, the book she dedicated to Violet, in a strange gipsy language, and in which she and Violet were depicted as the lovers, Julian and Eve.

The reality was fantasy, fantasy reality. Vita and Violet became in real life Julian and Eve; they were also Dmitri and Alushka. Julian was the tall and slender young man who sauntered the streets of London and Paris with his best girl on his arm; as the Grand Duke Dmitri, he claimed unrivalled *droit de seigneur*. No ordinary language could possibly convey everything the lovers wished to say, and they invented their own, based on a bizarre gipsy dialect. Gipsies represented the supremely romantic way of life that was their ultimate design: to be free to wander the world at will, unrestricted by ties of any sort, except to each other. Vita had of course a genuine though faint strain of gipsy blood; her grand-mother Pepita Duran had inherited gipsy blood from her mother, Catalina Ortega.

With fine disregard for their reputations, Vita and Violet lived their fantasies. Vita, as Julian, disguised herself as a soldier with a bandage round her head, but Violet made no attempt at disguise, and doubtless would have scorned to do so. To flaunt her love before the dull, self-satisfied world was her aim; had she been able to hire an aeroplane and write 'Violet loves Vita' across the skies, she would probably have done so. It is horrifying to think how easily the story could have been exposed: meeting at Hyde Park Corner of all places, taking taxi-rides together, and, later, drinking and dancing cheek-to-cheek in the cafés of Paris and Monte Carlo. Violet, in her fashionable frocks, much photographed as a dé-butante, was an easily recognisable figure to any enterprising reader of gossip pages. But luck was on their side, for the time being at least, combined perhaps with the fact that London and Paris were full of wounded soldiers, and the hats of the time brought about a certain anonymity. Pulled well down, the cloche made one woman look very much like another.

In July, the lovers stayed for another three weeks in Polperro, but meanwhile, Violet had transmitted all her love of foreign lands to Vita, and they both wished to broaden their horizons. It was hard to resist Violet at her most inspired.

'Mitya, think of the life we could have together exclusively devoted to the pursuit of beauty, beauty of form, beauty of colour, beauty of sound, beauty of composition, beauty in clay, in bronze, in marble, beauty in strange landscapes, in forgotten dwelling places, beauty uncouth, primitive, uncivilised – ah Mitya, chapes-car!* What have we to do with the vulgar, prattling, sordid life of

* Their gypsy word meaning 'escape'.

today? What care we for the practical little soigné occupations of our contemporaries. You *know* we're different – Gypsies in a world of "landed gentry".

'You, my poor Mitya, they've taken you and they've burnt your caravan, they've thrown away your pots and pans and your half-mended wicker chairs, they've pulled down your sleeves and buttoned up your collar! They've forced you to sleep beneath a self-respecting roof with no chinks to let the stars through – but I, Mitya! They haven't caught *me* yet – I snap my fingers in their faces! Come away, Mitya, come away, when they're all asleep in their snug white beds. I'll wait for you at the crossroads. . . .'[3]

In November, they left for Paris, and then travelled south to Monte Carlo, where they stayed until the middle of March 1919. Such a long absence, particularly since it covered Christmas, began to stir feelings of doubt in their families. Lady Sackville had thought it charming in April that Vita should be enjoying the flowers of a Cornish spring with Violet, but she thought it a great deal less charming that Harold Nicolson should have to spend Christmas alone with the two boys at Knole with his parents-in-law. By the beginning of 1919, in their separate ways, Mrs Keppel, Lady Sackville and Harold Nicolson were all uneasy. Mrs Keppel had allowed her elder daughter a great deal of freedom since she had come out, but now she thought the time had come for her to be safely married. A number of Violet's flirts had been killed in the war, but there was always Denys Trefusis, in whom Violet herself had once professed herself interested.

Violet and Denys shared many characteristics. Both highly intelligent, neither suffered fools gladly. They had the same sense of humour, the same sharp wit which Naomi Walford, Denys's niece, recalls being put to brilliant effect in a game of charades which reduced the whole company to howls of laughter. They both had a gift for languages and were particularly drawn to all things Russian. It was about now that Denys started to address Violet by the Russian form of her name, Fialka. In fact it was his Russian associations that had been one of his initial attractions: Russia that evoked unlimited freedom in her vast snowy steppes and unlimited romance in her literary past.

But even with so much in common, Denys was perhaps too detached a figure for such a wayward character, especially one who was deeply involved in a relationship she could not control.

With touching faith in the superiority of the male species and the rewards of a happy marriage, Mrs Keppel thought that once the ring was on Violet's finger, Denys would be able to control his capricious bride. She began actively to promote the match, conveying to Denys her conviction that all would be well after the ceremony and certainly putting forward attractive financial inducements.

But although he had no money of his own, Denys needed no such inducement. He was quite determined to marry Violet in the face not only of strong parental opposition, but also Violet's violent objections, culminating in a demand that if she did marry him, it was to be a marriage in name only, and that he was not to touch her.

The more she rejected him, the keener he became to marry: such is the contrary nature of love. And there was no doubt that his experience in the trenches had made him dependent upon her. She had come to represent to him out in France everything he was fighting for, a focus, a motive. If he had been aimless before, he more than made up for it now. Nothing was going to deter him.

Nor were the marriage settlements of much interest or consolation to the Trefusis parents who found it hard to be enthusiastic about their son's choice of bride. There were many girls in love with Denys, and it was horrible for his mother to think he was being made unhappy by one who struck her as unstable and over-emotional. When Violet sobbed at the opera during a performance of *Boris Godunov*, her future parents-in-law turned away disapprovingly.

The Trefusises had had a bad year as far as their sons' marriages went. Denys's elder brother, Kerr, who was very shy and withdrawn and had always adored Denys, had after the war gone to work as the business manager to a rich widow, a Mrs Alberta Mary Ellis. At first, his letters home contained anecdotes of this lady's fabled meanness – how she would mark the levels on the sherry and wine bottles so that she could check that none of her household was taking a surreptitious glass. But abruptly the anecdotes stopped and then came a staggering announcement that Kerr was engaged to his employer. Alberta Mary had been born in 1861, the same year as Mrs Trefusis! And when Kerr married in April 1919, his bride insisted on a white wedding, remembered to this day by Denys's niece, Naomi, who was the unfortunate bridesmaid to the anti-quated and rather overweight lady who presented a ludicrous sight even to Naomi's childish eyes.

As for Violet, there were many reasons why she finally agreed to become engaged to Denys, but she hated herself for it. Her mother had always been able to bring out the best in her, and it was very hard not to respond when she was firing every gun in her formidable battery of charm to make Violet agree. Violet's best friend, Pat Dansey, was also on Mrs Keppel's side and it seemed that Vita herself wanted her to marry Denys. Then there was Denys himself, cutting such a pathetic figure, and Violet was not so lost in self-pity that she could not spare some for him. A few days before her engagement was announced, at the end of March, she wrote sadly to Vita, trying to justify her action and evoking memories of past delights that she hoped could not fail to arouse Vita to some kind of useful prohibitive action.

'My own sweet love,

'I am writing this at 2 o'clock in the morning at the conclusion of the most cruelly ironical day I have spent in my life. This evening I was taken to a ball of some 700 people. Chinday had previously told all her friends I was engaged, so I was congratulated (!) by everyone I knew there. I could have screamed aloud. Mitya, I can't face this existence. I shall see you again on Monday, and it depends on you whether we ever see each other again. Mitya, it is really wicked and horrible. I am losing every atom of self-respect I ever possessed. I *hate* myself. O Mitya, what have you done to me, o my darling, precious love. What is going to become of us?

'I want you every second and every hour of the day, yet I am being slowly and inextricably tied to somebody else.

'Mitya, we *must* break away, or Heaven knows what might happen.

'O Mitya, I want you so. Sometimes I am flooded by an agony of physical longing for you such as I have never experienced in my life

– a craving for your nearness and your touch. At other times I feel I should be quite content if I could only hear the sound of your voice. I find myself beginning to say "Mitya" a hundred times a day. My love and my life, *come back to me*. I hold out such empty arms – I try

Violet's sketch of herself and Vita
as Eve and Julian in Paris

so hard to imagine your lips on mine – never was there such a pitiful imagining. . . .

'Your lovely tulips are at the foot of my bed – bless you for having sent them. . . .

'O my darling, whatever it may cost *us*, tiri Chinday* won't be cross with you anymore. I suppose this ridiculous engagement will set her mind at rest. Again I shut my eyes and pretend I can feel your arms around me – oh! but I can't, Mitya, I *can't* – to think tonight a week ago we were still at Monte Carlo! And I shall see you neither tomorrow, nor the next day – never was anyone more hungrily beloved – my lover, yes, I call you that, because you *are* that, you are more than anyone has ever been, or could ever be to me. Even if I lived to be a thousand, nothing and no-one in the world could kill the love I have for you.

'I have surrendered my whole individuality, the very essence of my being to you. I have torn the veils from the inmost shrine of my soul for your delectation. I have given you my body time after time, to treat as you pleased, to tear in pieces if such had been your will – all the hoardings of my imagination I have laid bare to you. There isn't a recess in my brain into which you haven't penetrated. I have clung to you and caressed you and slept with you, and I would like to tell the whole world. I clamour for you and *demand* you with all the force of love and youth and passion.

'I have more right to you than anyone in this world. You are my lover and I am your mistress, and kingdoms and empires and governments have tottered and succumbed before now to that mighty combination – the most powerful in the world. . . .'[4]

But Vita, once she was sure that Violet would remain faithful to her, was on balance in favour of the marriage. It would put paid to the gossip that had begun in shocked whispers. Then Violet, as a married woman, would be a great deal more independent than as a *jeune fille* living at home, under the increasingly watchful eye of her mother. There was, of course, Harold. Vita was not convinced that she was prepared to give him up completely and forever and she could therefore hardly expect Violet to defy her parents in order to remain free when she herself was tied. Lady Sackville, a tender but tactless mother, was bringing pressure to bear, both directly by speaking to Vita, and indirectly by adding to the flying rumours, referring to Violet as that 'arch-fiend'.

* i.e. Lady Sackville.

As for Mrs Keppel, as an Edwardian through and through, she minded not so much what was happening in private but that society at large should know. What counted was not what one did, but how one did it. As a generously well-adjusted woman herself, she probably did not understand her daughter's violent involvement with another woman, but what she did understand, only too well, was that her adored elder daughter was fast ruining herself in the eyes of the world. Once safely married, and far away on a protracted honeymoon tour, she felt sure that Violet would see the Vita episode in its true perspective. In the months that followed, she was to see the marriage as the terrible mistake it was, but for the time being it scotched the rumours. Nothing could have been more conventional than the grand wedding she was planning, though the bride was writing furiously to her lover, 'I feel like setting fire to St George's, Hanover Square'.

As for the lover's husband, it is to his credit that he saw Violet's engagement as an act of enormous self-sacrifice on her part, as the end of a relationship which could not continue. On 27th March 1919, the day after the engagement was announced, he wrote to her:

'My dear Violet,

'I have just got your letter which has distressed me terribly. It is horrible to think of the suffering you are going through – and the torture it must be to you to see friends and receive congratulations when your heart is heavy and your life seems utter loneliness and despair. . . . But I know that there is nothing to be done. I know that a love like yours requires everything or nothing, and that petty palliatives and temporary compromises only increase the despair. I know also that Vita is crushed under the sorrow of it and has scarcely the strength left to take any decision. So that it remains for me to decide – and I can only decide in one way. You cannot but see that I am right in doing this; it is not a question of convention and generosity, it is a question of wisdom and sympathy. You talk of ceasing to exist – and I know that you mean it. But Violet think what it would be to Vita if you darkened her life by such an action? In this tragedy you have won Vita's love forever – don't throw it away in a transitory despair.'

Perhaps Vita had not been completely honest with her husband, perhaps she really thought at this stage that once Violet was married, she would let her go. To her surprise, she found Denys a sympathetic character, as she related to her husband, in a letter dated 21st May 1919.

'I can't tell you how much I like him. I really really do. We had the most animated discussion. The whole way through dinner about everything under the sun – no personalities. He is very intelligent and not a bit banal. I do wish he was just a stray friend and not engaged to V.'

But as the wedding day drew closer, the strain began to show. Violet became distraught with horror at her own behaviour. What price beauty and freedom now? Lies and deceit, and the victory of convention were the order of the day.

'What is going to happen? Are you going to stand by and watch me marry this man? It's unheard-of, inconceivable. I belong to you body and soul, I ache for you all day and all night. You are my whole existence – O Mitya, it is so *horrible*, so *monstrous*, so *criminal*, to be with someone one doesn't care for, when one's whole being cries out for the person you *do* love, and *do* belong to. In all my life I have never done anything as wrong as this – you know how I loathe and abominate deceit and hypocrisy. To my mind, it is the worst thing on earth and here I am putting it all into practice – all the things I have most loathed and denounced to you *sur tous les tous* as being unworthy of you and I. O God, Mitya, what am I coming to – what can I do, what can I do? How can I get out of it, what am I to say? *Je me fais horreur* – I no longer feel clean and free, what is this hideous farce I am playing? If we could go away, you and I, even for a few months, I would get out of it, but if I got out of it, and remained here alone and without you, my life would be unendurable. My Chinday would make everything hell for me.

'O Mitya, you *must know* how repugnant it is to me to tolerate this relationship – it is *absolutely contrary* to all my ideas of morals. I mayn't have many, but this absolutely does them in. I hover between indescribable self-loathing and plans of suicide. . . .'[5]

Vita, typically, dissociated herself, leaving the scene of the intended crime and going to join Harold, who was a member of the British delegation at the Peace Conference in Paris. Paris! The place where Julian and Eve had strolled hand-in-hand, madcap, free and young. It was a betrayal.

Mitya, at night when you drive in the motor to your grand dinner-party, look out as you turn the corner – your chauffeur will nearly run over two crouching figures, arm-in-arm, who are preparing to cross. . . . *'Fais donc attention, grand fou!'* she says and she laughs up into his face. . . . They are standing under a *réverbère* – Good God! No, it can't be! Your imagination is playing you some trick – and yet – the motor is held up by traffic, you can examine them at your leisure. Poor things! They are obviously in love, and so *débraillés*, so down-at-heel – he with his red belt, hat pulled jauntily over one ear, she with her little, neat, black, frayed, *midinette* looking *tailleur*, with a bunch of violets tucked into her belt, – but why poor? They look so blatantly, ecstatically happy, look! They are whispering and laughing together at you, in your grand motor. *'Ils m'ont l'air fichtrement cossu, les bourgeois? – t'as pas envie d'en être, dis un peu?'* He teases her, she sentimental: *'Non, tu sais, ils me font toujours plus pitié qu'envie, ces gens là. Je suis sûre qu'ils ne savent pas ce que c'est que d'être heureux, d'être libre et jeune et poète. . . .'* Her voice dies away, the motor in front of you has moved on. You lean back with a gasp – you had recognized them – it wasn't your imagination – they were ghosts – you look anxiously at someone to see if he has noticed your perturbation – what it is to be a murderer! – Julian, Julian and Lushka.[6]

Vainly, Violet sought for reassurance. Harold, or someone, or Monsieur Un Tel as she called him, she dismissed. His diplomatic life did not interest her, to Violet it was too middle-class, too worthy, to take seriously.

'Take care, Mitya, if you love me, don't try to be too hard just at present. I'm on the brink of a precipice – the slightest push would send me over – you write literary, beautifully polished letters, with melodious flawlessly turned sentences – why don't you curse and rant and rave? Why won't you curse the blasted Fate that's taken you away from me, why don't you curse the malignant Fate that

keeps me crying for you night after night. Vigour! where's your
vigour? Passion! where's your passion? You're not made for vigour
and passion – anybody's only got to look at your neat rounded little
handwriting to be convinced of that – they've only got to look at
your beautiful, immovable face, your dignified, impersonal
manner! *Stick to your role*, Mitya, it's too late now – don't be a
renegade, continue to be changelessly beautiful and blamelessly
good! Continue to be intellectual, and well-informed, literary and
unemotional. Ça te va même très bien! Leave the dregs to me – to be
an outlaw and a rebel, leave it to me to be inaccurate, exorbitant,
jealous, egotistical, heartbroken, *fichue*, mad!

'Ce n'est pas ton genre, Mitya. I tried to make you like me, and
failed, I tried to make myself happy, and failed, I tried to make my
life a success – a permanent one – and failed again. My life – what is
left of it – is just one raw limitless bitterness – what can you expect?

'No, Mitya, be happy, but not *too* happy, because that would
be undignified, in the same way as it is undignified to be too sad.

'You will lead a happy, successful uneventful brilliant life –
probably ending up by being the wife of an ambassador! Dazzling
prospect! When you are old, you will look back upon your youth
and think: well, yes! I had one very strong temptation, but, thank
God! I was able to resist it.

'In Paris you will be taken to see artists, and artists' studios – you
will associate with literary and artistic people (someone will see to it
that you don't only have to do with bores). You will talk art and
poetry; people will say witty, brilliant things, a man called, I think,
Jean Cocteau, notably. You will think: how wrong Lushka was in
imagining I lead the ordinary, conventional life of a diplomat's wife!
Look at me now, in a real Bohemian milieu! *Good God alive*, Mitya!
But a *real* studio in which *real* Bohemians lived – not merely *les
arrivés* – would all put on clean clothes to receive the wife of a Peace
Delegate! You can't have your cake and eat it! Either you would be
'pigging it' on two or three hundred a year in a rive gauche attic with
me, perhaps not even that, uncertain as to when you were going to
have your next meal – or else, you've the other thing, the wife of a
Peace Delegate, beautiful, ambitious, prosperous, influential – but
you can't be both! Don't you make any mistake about that – and

there's no doubt as to which you have chosen, is there? Alas, alas, the iron has eaten into my soul, Mitya.

'. . . They have taken you away from me, Mitya, they have taken you back to your old life, *you who are so prone to take fakes for the genuine article.* You will think you are catching glimpses of Bohemian life now. My poor Mitya . . . it was Julian, not you, and Julian is dead.

'Remember what I said – it's the truest thing I've ever said about you – you are so prone to take fakes – faked *people* – for the genuine article. You don't *know* the genuine when you see it, you who are so critical, you have been taken in time after time. Taken in by me, you think I'm clever, *and I know I'm not*, but had you come to me, *I would have had genius.*

'I am filled with a rage of self-destruction now, a sort of moral suicide – you could have made anything of me, I could have walked among the stars. . . .

(Sunday morning) 'It is a lovely day. I wonder what you will do – you're so far away, *so* far away. Figurative mountains, oceans and continents separate you from me. As it's Sunday, someone will probably get the day off, and will naturally spend it with you. You probably won't write to me today, because you won't have time, and you won't be alone.

'You will wear your most becoming clothes, and look lovely. You will probably go and sit in somebody's room, while he changes his clothes – like you did when I was in Paris.

'And he will say: My little Mar and kiss the back of your neck.

'*Tu me fais horreur, Mitya, parfois tu me fais horreur.* The depths of duplicity in you make my hair stand on end.

'O Mitya, I *am* so unhappy, it's because I'm so unhappy I can't help writing all this. I am simply tortured with misery, the misery of missing you and knowing you in Paris, and jealousy. I don't mean what I say about duplicity, it's my horrible imagination that poisons everything and runs away with me. On the contrary, Mitya, you, knowing how hideously unhappy I am, won't surely be cruel enough to do things I should hate?

'O Mitya, I *do* love you so. Try to realise how dreadful everything is for me.

'Hugh lunched with me the other day; he is just going to Polperro – this time last year *we* were going—
'. . . Ah Mitya, don't forget me – you forget so easily.
'I saw Rosamund the other day, she looked so old, and sad. I shuddered. Will I be sent to join Rosamund some day? Ronsard me célébrait au temps où j'étais belle. . . .
'Plains moi un peu, Mitya;
'Je t'aimerai toujours.'[7]
Meanwhile the inexorable machinery of a big social wedding was under way. *The Times* of Saturday, 14th June 1919, carried an impressive list of presents to the bride, headed with a diamond brooch bearing the royal cipher from the King and Queen. Colonel Keppel gave his daughter a gold-fitted dressing case, and a writing-set; her mother gave her a diamond bandeau and a pearl necklace. More diamonds, this time combined with emeralds in a brooch, came from her aunt and uncle, the Earl and Countess of Albemarle, and the staff of 16 Grosvenor Street presented her with a silver inkstand.
The wedding took place on June 16th:
'There was a large company at St George's, Hanover-square . . . for the marriage of Captain Denys R. Trefusis, M.C., son of Colonel the Hon. John and Mrs Trefusis, and Miss Violet Keppel, elder daughter of Lieutenant Colonel the Hon. George and Mrs Keppel.
'On the bride's arrival at the church, the Corporal of the Horse in charge of the N.C.O.'s of the Royal Horse Guards forming the guard of honour presented her with a handsome bouquet tied with the regimental colours. She was accompanied by her father, who gave her away, and she wore a gown of old Valenciennes over chiffon, the train of which was of gold brocade with a raised pattern of velvet flowers. The veil was of soft tulle, and her ornaments included a pearl necklace given to her by her mother.'[8]
The report went on to describe the pages and bridesmaids (the chief of whom was Sonia) who 'were dressed in yellow chiffon with sashes of blue and silver and blue wreaths in their hair. The children wore Romney costumes in a similar shade of yellow.' Among the list of guests appears the name of Sir Ernest Cassel

whose shrewd advice had had such fortuitous results. Dame Nellie
Melba sang Gounod's "Ave Maria" during the signing of the
register.

Two of the children in attendance were Cecilia Keppel and
David McKenna who, fourteen years later, married each other.
Lady Cecilia recalls very little of the wedding itself, only the luncheon party Mrs Keppel gave at Grosvenor Street the day before,
following a rehearsal at the church. The food was wonderful, and
included, to a child's eye, magic-looking pastry boats filled with
scrambled egg.

The hateful honeymoon, starting in Paris, showed all three,
Violet, Denys and Vita, in the worst possible light: Violet viciously
cruel in her unhappiness, Vita violently destructive in hers, and
Denys cringing between them. Scarcely can the Ritz Hotel in Paris
ever have had such a strange pair of travellers on their *voyage de
noces*: the wife watching from her open bedroom door her lover
dining alone downstairs, while the husband wept in the
background. It was an intolerable situation.

Vita went to the Ritz to see Violet the day after she arrived.

'She was wearing clothes I had never seen before, but no
wedding ring. I can't describe how terrible it all was – that meeting,
and everything. It makes me physically ill to write about it and think
about it, and my cheeks are burning. It was dreadful, dreadful. By
then I had left Versailles, and was living alone at a small hotel. I
took her there, I treated her savagely, I made love to her, I had her,
I didn't care, I only wanted to hurt Denys, even though he didn't
know of it. I make no excuse, except that I had suffered too much
during the past week and was really scarcely responsible.'[9]

The marriage never stood a chance. Vita had been prepared to
stay safely out of the way while Violet married Denys, but she was
not prepared to stay indefinitely out of the way to see if they could
make anything of it. As for Violet, she realised, a week after the
wedding, that nothing had changed, that the same loathsome
situation existed, but with one difference: Denys.

'Try to think only of luncheon parties, clothes, luxury, flirtations,' she wrote to Vita from the Ritz on 23rd June. 'Be *small*, you
who were so unlimited. It is much better; it pays to be small.

Substitute Deauville for Tahiti, amourettes for amour, dilettantism for poetry, amusement for romance. I can't, I can't, I won't, so long as I live. Oh give me back my freedom. A lark with clipped wings. I feel desperate. The rows have begun worse than ever; we have been odious to each other. I can't help it. I don't care.'[10]

[4]
Prête à faire toutes les folies

Leaving Paris, the Trefusises travelled southwards, Violet endlessly trying to coerce Vita into some sort of responsible decision. Vita would not be honest, and Violet would not lie to Denys, not compromise in a state of affairs which she knew to be dishonest and despicable. 'I will not lie to L.* save in an absolute extremity. I know the truth hurts him frightfully, but I should feel absolutely beneath contempt if I lied to him . . . he is so essentially a person one cannot lie to.'[1]

But honesty does not necessarily bring harmony, and by the end of July, relations between Violet and Denys were no longer bitterly quarrelsome, just plain bad, although he seemed to want to help her, if he could.

Back in England, they took a house in Sussex called Possingworth Manor, from where Denys travelled daily (or sometimes stayed over the week) to London. He remained in the army until 1st April 1920 when he resigned his commission and was granted acting rank of Major on the Regular Army Reserve of Officers of the Royal Horse Guards. When Denys was away, Vita came over from Long Barn. The lovers were able to snatch moments of bliss together, relishing both spur of the moment visits and those that had been carefully planned. The physical want had not diminished.

'6.30

'Mitya, it's too awful: I can't sleep, I want you so, I have been lying awake for the best part of an hour, thinking of nothing else. I have opened the window wide, and the fresh, indescribably sweet air soothes my burning cheeks.

* L for Loge, their name for Denys Trefusis.

'I can't wait more than a day or two: we *must* have each other, it is brutal, imperative, and inevitable. Mitya, it is torture: yesterday afternoon was torture, every day that I see you, and can't have you, is torture. I must, I must.

'I told you at Monte Carlo it would end like this, in just the bare physical urgency. It *is* ending like this, for me. We are wasting time. We must waste time no longer.

'Damn you, Mitya, damn you for your colour, and your beauty, and your health, and your vitality – you make the most irresistible appeal to one's senses that it is possible to make.

'I almost hate you for it.

'Heavens above! The reason why I'm so jealous of you is obvious enough! If you weren't so damned attractive physically, do you think my heart would beat almost to suffocation whenever I see you speak to someone?

'If you don't realise how attractive you are in that way, let me tell you, other people *do*, and have told me so. . . .

'You simply *drain* everybody else of colour and life and movement. Look at Mrs Montagu,* she's supposed to be and probably *is*, extremely attractive. Look at Mrs Montagu next to you – a stuffed doll! Look at Loge! An automaton! If the room were chock full of lovely women, and you came in suddenly, people would think: this is the *real* thing!

'I'm not saying all this because I happen to be in love with you – but there is something about you, an outdoor, open-air, *borrowed* voluptuousness, as though you had just come in from the vineyards . . . "sweet upon the mountains", something indefinable that makes one think of the sap rising in the trees, then one realises abruptly and alarmingly that all life, and youth, and spring is boiling and effervescing in you – *l'appel à l'amour* – and everybody looks suddenly wan and old, like people who have been dancing all night look in the pitiless light of dawn.

'*That* is what makes you so different from everybody else. And o Mitya! you are so essentially pagan, "classically" pagan?! (Not

*Venetia Montagu, wife of Edwin and a close friend of the Prime Minister, H.H. Asquith.

always.)

'Mythological: I adore you for it. You sweep me (lit. and fig.) off my feet!

'You ought to have altars in the vale of Thessally, and each spring a ram without blemish, and a pure virgin (if there be such a thing!) would be sacrificed to you! And their blood would spurt ravishingly all over the assistants and Mitya, artiest of gods, would murmur: How Walter Pater!'[2]

But the gossip had started again, worse than ever, and it was imperative that there should not be an open scandal. According to Denys's parents, it was 'practically common property' that Denys was trying to get a separation from Violet, and Mrs Keppel and Denys were unanimous in trying to prevent Violet going abroad with Vita again. Nevertheless, the lovers did go away in October, again to Monte Carlo, a place Violet would never be able to visit again without pain. In later life, she always maintained she loathed the Côte d'Azur, doubtless because of the memories it evoked.

By the New Year of 1920, Violet's position was unenviable. She was beginning to know what it was to live in the *demi monde*, and she did not like it. A great deal of talk was circulating. It was imperative to escape permanently.

In early February, Vita finally made her decision. She would elope with Violet and they would make their lives together on the continent. On their way to the station, Violet read a letter from Denys describing his utter desolation. It failed to touch her, but awoke in Vita such a feeling of guilty remorse that she persuaded Violet to leave on the first leg of the journey alone. Violet sailed for France, and Vita remained overnight in Dover. She encountered Denys, who was following Violet. An uneasy friendship struck up between the two rivals and by the time they had undergone a vile crossing on the boat, a half-joking camaraderie existed. This bond was strengthened on arrival at Calais by the appearance of a stricken Violet, mentally and physically at a complete loss. United by their concern, Vita and Denys took her to an hotel and put her to bed. It is a most sympathetic image of Violet: propped up in that hotel bed in Calais with Vita and Denys discussing poetry and art across her, all three dining there in the room, Violet holding court like a cherished princess with her two devoted courtiers just that once in harmony. That they could all behave like this goes a long way towards making bearable the fearful scenes of recrimination that followed.

Seeing that the situation was hopeless, Denys returned to England and the lovers travelled to Amiens. At this stage, the Keppels and Lady Sackville stepped in, determined to prise them apart permanently. Violet's sister, Sonia, had become engaged to Roland Cubitt, and his parents, highly respectable, were not very favourably disposed towards the match. They did not care for the old Edward VII associations, and the Keppels knew that any more scandal attached to Violet would put paid to all Sonia's hopes.

Harold Nicolson enlisted the help of his mother-in-law, who suggested he should talk to Denys. Lady Sackville had had an interview with Denys at the beginning of the month, during the course of which he had admitted that he loathed Vita because she took Violet away from him. He had also told her that Violet was very fond of him physically, and that he was 'her husband absolutely'. Vita had told her mother that Violet was a virgin, and refused to have anything to do with her husband. Lady Sackville did not know whom to believe.

On arrival at Grosvenor Street, Lady Sackville found Denys preparing to fly to Amiens the following day. 'I asked him to take Harold as he had a two-seater aeroplane, and he most readily said he would. I took him to Cadogan Gardens where he saw Harold and arranged everything with him. Denys was very cold and collected, and fully determined to bring Violet back or have done with her.'[3]

In 1920, Amiens was little changed from the time of the great 1918 offensive. In the cathedral, the shattered stained glass windows were still boarded up and the countryside around the city was apparently irrevocably scarred by war: roads made almost impassable by shells, bordered by naked tree-trunks on which there were no signs of new life, by windowless, roofless houses and occasionally Army huts and an old casualty clearing station.

We, whom the storm-winds battered, come again
Like strangers to the places we have known,

> Who sought men's understanding all in vain
> For hardened hearts to grief's dark image grown. . . .[4]

It is painful to think of Denys in that place of unbearable memories
with all the horrors of his personal hell. And the interview that took
place that day in Amiens was grotesque, displaying all the
protagonists in a loathsome light, a five-part drama which cul-
minated in Denys telling Vita – truly or falsely – that Violet was
'really' his wife, that he had made love to her. Vita stormed away to
Paris with Harold. Violet persuaded Denys to take her there. She
swore to Vita that Denys had lied, but Vita lost faith. This was the
crisis, and the relationship suffered a mortal blow from which it
finally died a slow and lingering death.

From an obdurate Vita, Denys took his heartbroken wife south.
They were to meet the Keppels at Toulon. En route, Denys, whose
health since the war had been extremely poor, nearly died. The
distracted chauffeur rushed between the hotel and the chemist for
quinine and aspirin. Violet was frozen with despair: '*Je suis prête à
faire toutes les folies*'. Frantic with lost hopes, she could not look
after Denys who ordered her out of his room on the rare occasions
she went in.

At Toulon, worse awaited her. Mrs Keppel was immovable.
Although the marriage had been a 'hideous mistake', the only way
of saving face now was for Violet to travel round the world with
Denys. If she refused, her parents would have nothing more to do
with her, financially or otherwise. Denys threatened annulment,
and he was prepared to bring in Vita's name, putting forward
'undue influence'. The Keppels were horrified, but Violet tried her
uttermost to gain their consent. She offered, if they permitted the
annulment, to live at home with her parents. But Mrs Keppel
refused outright. 'She said I should never set foot inside her house,
and that she would never speak to me again. I went down on my
knees to her.'[5]

Eventually, the Keppels relented slightly, at least as far as going
round the world was concerned. Violet stayed on in the South of
France, losing heavily at the casino, and once when she met her
mother in Monte Carlo, her mother shook hands with her as if she

were the most casual acquaintance, cutting Violet to the heart. It all now depended on Vita; there were only two essentials, 'you and freedom. Life has become strangely simplified'.

Finally Vita relented towards Violet and consented to join her at Avignon. They travelled by way of San Remo to Venice, another place Violet was to dislike throughout her life because of its associations. In Venice, they found Pat Dansey with a friend, and this was the start of a strange rôle of go-between that Pat was to play in the aftermath of the love affair.

Back in London in April, Violet found herself barely on speaking terms with her parents. 'I had a letter from my father . . . apparently I've got to clear out of G. Street as soon as possible, as they don't want me to come here except on invitation.'[6] The Keppels did not want Violet in London at all; she was ruined socially, an embarrassment to her family, and it seemed that a quiet country existence was all that was left open to her. Denys found a house at Sonning-on-Thames – 'suburb of Reading', as Violet scornfully dismissed it. The Manor House was everything she loathed and, worst of all, she was dependent upon Denys. Any pity she had had for him had evaporated after Amiens; he had removed and burnt all Vita's letters to her, the very testament of Vita's love for her; he had wrecked her life, and she could never forgive.

'Do you realise that I shall never see anyone, anyone? That at Reading, I shall be entirely alone except for D? I don't think there is room to have anyone to stay, even if I were able to! It is prison – but even worse than anticipated – I shall get no kindness from my family. I am entirely dependent on him for that: if he adopts a charitable attitude, they will too, but not otherwise. I was never in such a position in my life. Fool, fool, *fool* that I've been to come back.

'I am perfectly *certain* I shall get no tolerance from him where you're concerned, certainly not for the present. My family will wait and see if I what they call "make good" before relenting.'[7]

The reality of The Manor House was almost laughable.

'I have just woken up in this absurd little house . . . I *cannot* live here: *c'est une manie comme une autre*. I absolute *abominate* small rooms and low ceilings. I can't believe this house wasn't built for a dwarf, it is so diminutive and that theory alone gives me the creeps. I feel the collapse of the beam over my bed is imminent. I shall probably go mad here. The low ceilings and tiny rooms will contract and contract until I am squashed to death (plot for grand guignol). I am not joking: small rooms terrify me.'[8]

As long as Vita was on her side, Violet thought she could take any privation. She had lost the security of her parents' love, her place in society, most of her friends, the love of her husband. But it was all worth it as long as Vita cared, as long as Vita kept coming to see her, as long as they could meet now and then, as long as there was the hope that one day they would escape.

There were awful days when doubt set in, and the terrible waste of their young lives struck Violet once again. What had their love become, she asked Vita in an undated letter in May, 'a debased crippled crafty thing, of furtive pleasures and *false* generosities, of mean impulses and steroid understanding. But to my mind, the worst thing of all is its flagrant, its crushing hypocrisy. Under our skilful perversion – *and not only ours but other people round us* – cowardice becomes prudence, selfishness is called love, misleading evasions are supposed to be "kindness". Meanness, blindness and jealousy are all different manifestations of "love" . . . it is impossible for *any* love to expand healthily under such circumstances; it must always be a shrivelled abortion. It has no air, no scope, no margin; in whatever direction it tries to spread itself it is immediately arrested by outside limitations of one kind or another. It is kept for weeks in the dark, once or twice a little sunlight is let in, just to prevent it from dying utterly . . . It is impossible to "make the best of" a life like this. How can one make the best of anything that revolves on lies and deception? No, everything must be cleared up, set straight and readjusted.'

Violet wanted Vita but she also wanted an end to a hypocritical life that disgusted her. To her, Vita's marriage to Harold, when she loved Violet, was a horrifying duplicity.

'Because you don't see things as I see them, because you don't *really* understand, you think I am wicked and selfish – so I am, according to your standards, but not according to my own. According to my own, I am singularly pure, uncontaminated, and high-principled. You will laugh, *but it is true*. And you can laugh all you like, but it will still be true.

'I am after something which you have just caught a glimpse of, but which is omnipresent with me.

'I don't know whether I shall ever succeed in making anyone see life as I see it, because it is the side of life they don't and won't see.

'I sit at the front of an invisible altar, and am dazzled by its freshness and its youth.'[9]

There was always hope, however, that they might eventually get away together. At the end of May, Violet received some news from Vita, that put her in high spirits: 'I think that was very good work on your part to have got H. to consent so soon. *Je te félicite, ma vieille branche. Ma quando??????* And what does "in principle" mean?'[10]

In her over-excited state, the constant promises of elopement, made probably more with a view to appeasement than with any real intention, were making Violet more and more unstable. She rocketed from the depths of despair to the heights of happiness. Meanwhile, the terrible waiting was a sacrilege to the purity and freedom of their love.

'We are making a sort of brawling tavern out of what was once a Greek temple. All day long half-drunken people bawling obscene refrains stagger under its crumbling friezes; where garlanded youths and maidens once danced rapturous dances to the spring, ignoble old men throw dice for money. . . .

'And we stand by and do nothing. Soon it will be ruined irretrievably . . . *je suis triste à mourir*. Everything is being desecrated, profaned, trampled on. It is *shocking*. . . .

'The only really effective thing would be to transplant our temple, stone by stone, and set it down in some new site. . . . Failing that, we must turn out the drunkards, gamblers, usurers and thieves which inhabit it at present.'[11]

The months passed in a dreary succession, enlightened sometimes by evasive promises from Vita. Not the least part of the misery lay in the fact that Vita was surrounded by love and affection and Violet, banished to Sonning, was alone. The love affair had become her whole existence.

'My future seems to be solitude in hotels. Hotels I don't object to, but I loathe solitude. What I do mind, acutely, devastatingly, is having no friends, no-one who really cares what becomes of me, whether I am happy or not. You will say that you care. I am sure you do; but life is so different for you. You are surrounded by people who care for your comfort and happiness, people who will never fail you. Do you realise how lucky you are? There is nothing permanent in my life.'[12]

There was too the agony of her estrangement from her mother, the person after Vita whom Violet had loved most and for longest.

'I know you realise how intensely I feel about my mother. I could not live in the same country as she was, knowing that by living either with you (which would end in disaster) or near you, I was insulting her more and more irrevocably, and making her hate me more and more each day.'[13]

At the end of July 1920, Denys Trefusis nearly died of influenza, a crisis which precipitated yet another promise from Vita that she would have the ultimate talk with Harold, telling him that she meant to live abroad permanently with Violet. In her frantic state, Violet was completely unable to nurse or sympathise with her husband as he lay almost at death's door. This was perhaps one of the reasons why in August he again started threatening proceedings, 'with the fullest publicity'. Aghast, with Sonia's wedding planned for November, Mrs Keppel wrote a hard letter to her elder daughter, pointing out the odium and shame of becoming Miss Keppel again. Violet sent a scrap of the letter to Vita; still she did not react. An uneasy lull settled over them all; they were all waiting to see what Denys and Vita would do after Sonia's wedding. Violet went unwillingly to Duntreath with her mother. They had a curiously happy time, Mrs Keppel unbending towards her recalcitrant child who retreated into the fastness of her childish memories of blissful holidays so many years before. 'I am terribly against being grown up,' she wrote to Vita on 24th August, 'It does nobody any good.'

From Scotland, they went to Clingendaal but now the strain on Mrs Keppel was beginning to show. She spent whole days out walking in the damp woods, and at meals was so outspokenly rude to Violet that Lady de Trafford, who was also staying, was moved to

Vita and her two children at Long Barn

expostulate. Never had Violet been treated like this. From the cradle onwards, the curly-headed, dimpled darling of the house had been flattered and encouraged. Now she hardly dared open her mouth for fear of Mrs Keppel's wrath. Even George Keppel remonstrated with his wife, but her heart was set. Denys Trefusis, weak and ill, was living in a hut in the grounds, probably with suspected tuberculosis. He did not address a single word to his wife. Violet was alone, and time was flying.

'Youth will have gone as irrevocably as this summer, and all our tears and supplications won't bring it back. Across my life only one word will be written, "waste", waste of love, waste of talent, waste of enterprise. What could be worse or more despairing?'[14]

She tried hard to concentrate on a novel she was writing (which she never appears to have finished) but her concentration was far away, and besides she was convinced she could only write when she was happy. What would Vita make of her manuscript?

'Now I wonder about my book: it is *so* rotten in places. What *will* you say?!! . . . It depresses me to think of its probable reception at your hands.

'You know I said yours was sensual? Mine isn't, it is suggestive, which is worse. Yours is like a person with no clothes on, and mine is like a person with . . . one garment, completely inadequate as to length and breadth, and completely transparent.'[15]

Back in Sonning in November, Violet's pulses were racing with the thought of freedom, the south, the sun and escape.

'I crawled down here in a motor, at the rate of about 5 miles an hour, as the fog was so dense. How do you like the English winter? . . .

'This morning I went to see the Spanish pictures. I liked the old ones, and adored the moderns; they have the most amazing vitality. In that fog-laden atmosphere they were a protest and a challenge. We must go together – they are redolent of the south especially the moderns – and over everything that *tawniness*, that liver-colour that one only gets in Spain, and the desert.

'I loved the little gitanas, brown as berries, with shiny blue-black heads; the lean, graceful matadores, the bleached sierras, the cruel, blue-chinned priests, with here and there the scarlet splash of a cardinal's robe, the whining squalor of beggars, the contorted iron balconies, sly accomplices of intrigue, the fat old ladies with moustaches, and a leer.

'I even loved the old masters, Zurbaran, Velazquez, Ribera, El Greco: their dignity, and menace, and contempt!

'What aristocrats they were, all those people, what panache, what magnificence!

'The men with their long mournful faces, dressed more often than not in unrelieved black, the women erect, sedate, ugly – yet withal, indescribably *grandes dames*! I would have liked a hidden orchestra playing 'Pavane pour une infante défunte' for the old masters, and for the modern painters, the twang and beat of guitars playing a *jota* or a *seguidilla*, in a rather ominously uncommunicating circle . . . you know how they play, all hunched up and smoking and watchful. They are always one family and the niece, Pilarcita dances. . . .

'Pilarcita danced. She had a small sleek head; no comb or flowers, or anything. She had small skilful brown fingers that snapped and beckoned and rejected, all in turn. She was sixteen, and engaged to her cousin, Ramon, who played the guitar so sullenly. She had a lovely red shawl, with white blossoms embroidered on it. Her teeth were small – almost like *dents de lait* – and amazingly white in her pointed brown face. Pilarcita danced, and the blue smoke curled up in spirals from cigarettes – *ah volupté*. . . .'[16]

Reality was London, and Sonia's wedding in the middle of the month. Mrs Keppel, regally beautiful in black, with Egyptian embroidery in coral, gold and turquoise was far removed from salacious gossip, but the bride's sister was made of far softer material, and it hurt to be ignored. It hurt too when Christmas came, and her only present was a fur coat from Vita.

Then at the start of 1921, it seemed as if everything might work out after all. Vita did agree to go away once more, and they travelled that well-trodden path southwards, this time to Hyères and Carcassone. But it was far from their most blissful sojourn together. It had become impossible for the relationship to continue in isolation.

Perhaps a combination of Vita and Violet against the world

would have been powerful enough to withstand the massed allies of
Denys and Harold, Lady Sackville, and Keppel parents, with all the
weight of the disapproving Cubitts behind them, but the core of the
combination was irredeemably flawed since the crisis at Amiens.
And when lawyers were brought in, to extract promises, and
threaten, Vita cracked apart, and went back to everything she had
once chucked aside so impatiently: her children, her cottage, her
garden, her reputation, and particularly her husband. Not an
obvious choice for a tower of strength, this was nevertheless Harold
Nicolson's role, and his supporting actors and *mise en scène* made
almost equally strong appeals.

But Violet, how much less she had to lose, and how much more
she lost! No words could really describe her utter heartbreak in
losing Vita.

'I was so upset by what the lawyer told me that I nearly fainted in
the taxi coming home. When you say you'll give me up when I'm
down, knowing that it is indirectly owing to you that I'm brought so
low, I am hardly responsible at the moment – I might do anything
and you couldn't blame me. I simply don't know how to envisage
life without you. It doesn't seem worthwhile. If we separate, it will
be the end of everything.'[17]

But it was the end. Lady Sackville wrote in her diary on 10th
March 1921:

'I felt so upset when I saw V. that I appeared rather cold. I spoke
my mind very freely when we had our long talk which lasted till 2.
She says that V.T. is absolutely given up by everybody and
although she promises to do all she can to get rid of that friendship,
she can't very well drop her altogether and she must do it gradually.
She said she would be seen as much as she could with Harold. . . .'

At Grosvenor Street, Violet was imprisoned. Even letters were
censored and had to be smuggled out to the post. But what was the
point of smuggling them out, when they failed to touch the heart of
the person to whom they were addressed?

'I write to you in the deepest depression from this solemn house,
this inhuman, detached, disdainful house, which is so much more
the house that one would expect *you* to have . . . I write to you in a
little room which is too small to indulge in any of these attributes

except *en miniature*. Outside one hears the impersonal roar of traffic.

'I have never been so much alone as during the last three days. It is as though I had got acquainted with myself for the first time. I have never stayed with myself before. I don't like myself; I find myself a dull, exacting, pessimistic companion. I fill the house, myself eyes me coldly from every mirror, myself trails wearily after me, up and down a sneering staircase, in and out of contemptuous inadequately clad rooms. Pat brought a little warmth, a little life with her this afternoon, but the house paralysed our intimacy.

'It didn't say anything, it just sneered. . . .

'I am like the painful, difficult life that goes on beneath eight inches of ice. People skate heavily over me. Perhaps it will freeze right down to me, perhaps it will *freeze me in*? But my half petrified heart still stirs rebelliously from time to time. *It knows it suffers.*

'All this may sound funny to you, but I am writing with the utmost seriousness. When I realised you weren't coming my numbed heart just says O-h painfully, and a drop of frozen blood oozed slowly out of it, it is altogether too hurt, too stricken to move. . . . And Pat is going, and Mama has gone, and you are away. . . . I feel like the idiot in *Boris*. Can you hear the music, ending in a hopeless, helpless whine, almost animal, ageless, indefinite, imbecile?

'Presently, perhaps tomorrow, you will kick my heart, and it will die, frozen fast in pretty red icicles.'[18]

There was much more than loneliness and desolation to bear, however. There was the ghastly humiliation of a trip to Devonshire to the house of Denys's parents, a trip which misfired since it was undertaken with a view to Violet seeing Denys who had refused ever to see her again. Violet had with her a letter, couched in the humiliating terms of surrender, but a mile from the house, her mother-in-law sprang out of a ditch carrying a red lantern and signalling for the car to stop. She then loudly berated Violet in front of the chauffeur, and packed her back to where she was staying.

In the end, however, Denys did not annul the marriage, although it was months before he and Violet were on speaking terms. Totally alone, Violet was left to cope with the ruins of her life, with only Pat Dansey in the world to lend a sympathetic ear. Her beloved mother

had become an implacable figure without mercy. In May she went
with her to Rome. 'She says that her affection for me is irrevocably
dead, and that after S's baby is born, I may do what I like.' In June,
they were in Florence, not a success. Violet wrote to Pat prophetic
words as she left for Holland.

'As for Florence – !!! I have never hated a town so much. The
relief of not being able to see that tedious old Duomo, and those
sickly villas – those suburban hills is too great to be expressed. One
day, if I'm still alive, I shall write a book about Florence. It will be
vitriolic . . .'.[19]

From Clingendaal, she tried to be more optimistic, but it was an
effort.

'I feel as though I had been attacked by highwaymen, and left
bruised, naked and bleeding beside the roadside – and Fate
gleefully shouts: There! *Now* let's see what you can do. You had all
sorts of other defences, other protections, now you've only got
yourself. You've got your brain, and as a last resource, you've got
your body . . . but *you've got nothing else.* You don't know how
exposed I feel, but *one* other thing, I hope and trust I've got: the
love of the highwayman!'[20]

At the beginning of September, Pat Dansey wrote to Vita: 'You
mustn't be under the impression anyone is forcing V. to go back to
D. – it was entirely her own suggestion – and her mother refuses to
advise her one way or the other.'[21]

On what terms Violet made her peace with Denys, it is
impossible to know. Eventually they were able to settle down to a
more-or-less compatible familiarity. They were able to live
together, not in London where Violet was for the time being a
notorious figure, but in Paris, and the beauty of her favourite city
helped infinitely to ease the heartbreak. And so attached did she
become to France that she eventually decided to make it her home.

And in the end too Violet was reunited with her parents, and her
relationship with her mother emerged strengthened from the
terrible troubles it had suffered. Pat Dansey played a part in
bringing this about, and also in the reconciliation between Denys
and the Keppels which took place in May 1922. At a grand
luncheon party in Paris, paid for by Mrs Keppel, they made it up,

and all was forgiven and agreed to be forgotten.

But what had happened to the vagabond Violet, the laughing girl in her Mayfair dresses, shrimp-net in hand on the Cornish beaches, the romantic, radiant, glowing girl, dragging Vita by the hand through the streets of Paris, along the flower-starred paths of the South of France? What had become of the person who exclaimed:

'Freedom . . . romance! The world before us, to roam at will; fairs to dance at; strange people to consort with, to see the smile in their eyes, and the tolerant "Lovers!" forming on their lips. To tweak the nose of Propriety, to snatch away the chair on which she would sit down! Who in their senses would harness the divine courser to the mail-cart? . . . I'll own you before the world – and court its disapproval. I'll release you – no, I'll leave you – when you tire of me. I wouldn't clip love's golden wings. I wouldn't irk you with promises, blackmail you into perjury, wring from you an oath we both know was made only to be broken. We'll leave that to middle-age. Middle-age – I have been told there is such a thing? Sometimes it is fat, sometimes it is wan, surely it is always dreary! It may be wise and successful and contented. Sometimes, I'm told, it even loves. We are young. Youth! . . . the winged and the divine.'[22]

The vagrant gypsy had become a cruelly disappointed shadow of her true self. Everything she had held dear, all her burning ideals, she had betrayed. And worse still, Vita, the representative of those ideals, the pagan goddess of freedom, freedom to live a life dedicated to absolute beauty and absolute truth, had shown she had feet of clay. Safely ensconced at Long Barn, immersed in her *vie de famille*, she was lost forever to Violet.

The process of healing was an agonizingly slow one. The emotional scars would always show. The suffering Violet underwent shaped her into the woman she became, a woman never able again to give herself so completely, a whole-hearted dedication of self and spirit. Relationships with other people would always be tempered with reservation. Violet could never wholly commit herself again.

The heights had been sublime, but the depths were abysmal, and at the moment looked eternal.

[5]

Paris pouvait tout remplacer

Violet had made her first visit to Paris with her Aunt Jessie and Mademoiselle at the end of April 1905. She was not quite eleven and she kept a diary of her visit. Her childish heart was instantly captivated, and she recorded in her best handwriting going for a walk on the first afternoon in the Champs Elysées: '. . . it was too lovely, all the horse chestnuts were out and smelt so nice'. Indeed, she had at crack of dawn burst into Aunt Jessie's bedroom and announced: 'When I'm grown up, I'm going to live in Paris!'

And it was to Paris that this disillusioned, introspective woman came. It was the obvious solution: far enough from London to remove Violet from Vita, it was near enough for Mrs Keppel to keep a watchful eye over her difficult daughter.

In 1921 Denys was given a job in Paris in a bank or an insurance office, and he and Violet moved into a small flat in rue Fourcroy. Denys quickly found his feet in Paris, partly because, in the early 1920s, the French capital was full of Russian emigrés – mainly aristocrats as, for example, Prince Felix Yousoupoff (who had assassinated Rasputin), and others who had had to find employment as cab-drivers, night-club dancers, musicians and models at the famous couture houses. For Denys, who passionately loved that country and had acquired complete fluency in Russian since his time as tutor there (though probably the everyday language in such a household was French), anyone or anything Russian soon found a special place of affection in his heart. Years later, Violet said in a letter to Cyril Connolly, 'Russia was his Holy Land'.

Violet was jealous of Denys's friendships but at least jealousy was a more positive emotion than the dejected state into which she had fallen after the end of the love affair. She roused herself to take an interest in what he was doing, and if this led to some picturesque quarrels, at least it stopped the endless brooding.

One violent quarrel concerned the most beautiful mannequin at Chanel, Madame Ludmila Rubassof, with whom Violet discovered Denys to be having a love affair. When accused, Denys coolly retorted, '*Je n'étais pas fait pour le mariage. Et bien oui, je l'aime, Ludmila. C'est une femme exquise qui a eu tous les malheurs*'.[1]

After a year in rue Fourcroy, Denys and Violet exchanged their tiny flat for another in rue Laurent Pinchat. 'We were by no means unhappy there, and occasionally gave makeshift dinner parties.'

Inevitably though they led their own lives. Although this divergence could lead to some monumental disagreements, generally it led to a great deal more tolerant understanding. Denys's great love, after Russia, was music, a love which Violet was to a great extent able to share. Travelling on business, music, night-clubs, and sloe-eyed dancers frequently took him out of the flat and perhaps not being too much in each other's company made living together easier.

In 1923 a dream was realised when they found a house at Auteuil, in rue de Ranelagh. There was a lovely garden filled with trees, and the house itself was soon decorated in Violet's special way, a hotch-potch of different styles, periods and colours.

'There were Chinese rugs with geometrical patterns, Venetian mirrors full of reminiscences and plots, glass pictures, one of which was given me by my mother. It represented a Chinese lady smiling at a small grey parrot perched on her arm. She attempts nothing to detain it. Its cage is in her eyes.'[2]

Established at the rue de Ranelagh, Violet acquired a little of the peace of mind for which she had been searching for so long. The house provided a secure background from which she felt more confident about picking up the threads of a new life. She began to attend classes at the Sorbonne and, nearing 30, wrote a play called *Les soeurs ennemies* about Mary Queen of Scots and Elizabeth I. Although she had no close friends, her eyes were fully open to the infinite possibilities that Paris had to offer, and her intense love of her adopted country gave her the encouragement she needed in taking the first steps. *Je renonçai à renouer avec mon passé et me rebattai sur Paris. Paris pouvait tout remplacer: les amitiés tombées en désuétude, les démarches nécessaires pour en trouver de nouvelles.*[3] (I surrendered all my links with my past and began again in Paris. Paris would make up for everything: friendships fallen into disuse and the measures needed for making new ones.)

A new friend who was to become a very close one was someone to whom Violet said Denys had introduced her in 1923: Princesse Edmond de Polignac. Born Winnaretta Eugénie Singer on 8th January 1865, the princess was the seventeenth child fathered by Isaac Singer (the inventor of the sewing machine of the same name) and the first of his children to be both conceived and born in wedlock. Her mother was Isabelle Eugénie Boyer, a Frenchwoman whom Isaac Singer met in the summer of 1862. It was from her mother that Winnaretta probably inherited her love of music.

The little girl had a somewhat nomadic childhood. From the United States, which they left when Winnaretta was two, they went to Paris, where they lived for three years, until impending invasion from the Prussian army forced them to move to London, where Isaac Singer bought 32 Grosvenor Gardens. But London fog and the long English winters affected Isaac Singer's health and before long he decided to move to Paignton where he built an enormous house with a hundred rooms, inappropriately called 'The Wigwam'.

He did not have long to relish the joys of Paignton however as he died soon after The Wigwam was completed and Mrs Singer shortly afterwards returned to Paris with the children, now numbering six. There she married the Vicomte d'Estenburg et Duc de Camposelice, a member of the Luxembourgeois nobility. Elegantly established at 27 avenue Kleber, the Duchess began to hold musical evenings and concerts, sponsoring and encouraging in a small way the love of music which her daughter was so greatly to emulate in later years.

Meanwhile, relations between mother and daughter had begun to deteriorate. Winnaretta was a strange, introverted child, highly sensitive to music and to art, but oddly unreceptive to anything outside them. People found it difficult to penetrate her cold exterior, caused mainly by intense shyness. She looked rather

An early photograph of Winnaretta, Princesse de Polignac with her friends, a number of whom were later to become close friends of Violet. Marcel Proust, third from left, top row; Winnaretta Singer, centre of centre row; Anna, Comtesse de Noailles, right, centre row; the Princesse de Caraman-Chimay, front row.

formidable too: icy blue eyes, a thin-lipped mouth, and a jutting chin.

An unsuccessful first marriage in 1887 to Prince Louis de Scey-Montbéliard made her even more withdrawn. In 1891 there was a civil divorce, followed in February of the next year by an annulment from the Vatican.

Before her marriage, Winnaretta had developed strong lesbian tendencies which her husband made no attempt to understand, and his subsequent behaviour had shocked and horrified her. There could be no other outcome but divorce.

As an experience, the marriage had been thoroughly distasteful, but at least as Princesse de Scey-Montbéliard, she was now an independent woman who could lead her own life in the way she wanted, attending those gatherings that interested her, without having to ask permission of her mother. As heiress to an immense fortune, she was also able to give rein to her inordinate love of beauty in all forms, but particularly to the sustained patronage of unknown musicians and painters.

After the annulment, Winnaretta bought an enormous sombre house on the corner of avenue Henri-Martin and rue Cortambert. She immediately began complete works of reconstruction. The architect she employed was Grand'Pierre and on matters of interior decoration, she consulted Robert de Montesquiou. The final result was perhaps typical of such collaborators. A vast staircase led to the first floor which was used only for entertaining and on which was an enormous music room, so large that the two Steinway concert pianos in it looked lost.

By the end of 1892, some of Winnaretta's friends had decided that as an immensely rich divorcee of somewhat special tastes, she was at risk of becoming perhaps a little too well-known, and that she should marry again. They had, moreover, the perfect candidate in mind. This was an elderly prince of impeccable background, who possessed many attractive qualities. Much in demand as a guest, he was witty, intelligent and charming. Best of all, he was fanatical about music.

Winnaretta married Prince Edmond de Polignac on 15th December 1893. If cynics like Edmond de Goncourt recorded in their diaries, 'It is said that the marriage between these two was concluded on the condition that the husband does not enter his wife's room, on the payment of a sum of money which might permit him to mount his music which the opera houses do not want',[4] others, more charitably minded, could see that this ill-assorted couple (Winnaretta was 28, the prince 59) took a great deal of pleasure in each other's company and before long came genuinely to love each other. Theirs was a true marriage of minds: they shared many interests apart from music, and it was only when it came to the physical side of marriage that they agreed to go their own very individual ways.

Proof of the love the new princess held for her husband was her Christmas present in 1894: an immense palace in Venice, completely renovated, and renamed Palazzo Polignac.

This was the year when Violet was born in London and, in the intervening years, undeterred by the death of the prince in August 1901, the princess had unceasingly continued her generous patronage. Throughout the 1890s, she had held annual art exhibitions in her house in Paris and her salon had become established as the most intellectual of all, devoted entirely to the discussion of the arts and to all types of musical evenings.

Winnaretta was friend, patron and sponsor to most of the leading musicians of the time. She had helped and encouraged Fauré, Debussy, Delius and Ravel, and many others were to follow.

As she also owned a house in the King's Road, Chelsea, it is possible that she met Mrs George Keppel in London. The first record of their meeting, however, is in the spring of 1919, when both Mrs Keppel and the princess attended a dinner party given by Lady Colebrooke at the Ritz in Paris.

In 1906, Winnaretta met Diaghilev, who became a firm friend, and this friendship led to a close and happy involvement in the Russian ballet. She was one of the chief patronesses of the performance in May 1909, when 'A glittering cast of unknowns from the Maryinsky Theatre made such an impression that their names, Fokine, Bolin and Nijinsky, Ida Rubinstein, Pavlova and Karsavina soon went into household usage'.[5]

The involvement with the Russian ballet led to an involvement of a more intimate nature with Baroness Olga Alberta de Meyer. Olga Alberta was reputed to be an illegitimate daughter of Edward VII, by the Duchess di Caracciola. She certainly occupied a place of honour in a special box reserved for King Edward's particular favourites at his coronation in 1902. The ravishing Alice Keppel also had a seat in the box.

Another close friend of the princess was Romaine Brooks whom she had met in London in 1908, and who had fallen madly in love with Winnaretta, pursuing her to Paris. This painter later became famous for her portraits, mainly of women of inverted sexual tastes, such as Una Lady Troubridge, portrayed with monocle and dachshunds. There is reputed to be a painting of Violet Trefusis by Romaine Brooks, but if there is, it has disappeared without trace. In fact when she came to live in Paris, Violet had very little to do with the small band of well-known lesbians who flourished there. She found the whole set distasteful, and it is very unlikely that she would have sat for her portrait to one of its most notorious members.

By the time Winnaretta met Violet in 1923, the princess was 58 and a celebrated figure in European society, mainly because of her magnificent sponsorship of the arts, but also for her sharp tongue and snappy repartee. Most people came off worse in verbal encounters with this formidable figure, and many were the stories told about her. She was not, however, in the least intimidating towards Violet: an immediate attraction sprang up between the middle-aged princess and the lonely young wife. The initial attraction was fanned by mutual interests as, for example, the Russian ballet, which had greatly inspired Violet when she first saw it in London in 1912, and with which the princess had been closely involved since her introduction to Diaghilev in 1906. Apart from music and painting, they also shared a heightened sensitivity towards all forms of beauty. Because the princess was so rich, she was able to give to Violet and herself full rein in the pursuit of beauty, travelling afar in its search.

By 1923, when Denys Trefusis was said to have introduced his wife to the princess, there was little trace of the jealousy that had previously strained his feelings for Violet, and as he was no doubt aware of the direction in which the princess's tastes lay, if he did effect the introduction, he presumably knew what might happen. But Denys needed freedom and Violet needed distraction. She was bored and lonely and there was nothing in her life that even began to take the place of everything she had invested in Vita. She felt unloved and unlovable.

Denys seemed to have become the darling of the wasp-waisted Caucasian dancers and, on the rare occasions when Violet accompanied her husband to night clubs, she was left to watch, no doubt feeling very much on the side-lines, ignored and frumpy. For Violet was beginning to grow plump: someone nicknamed her '*Madame Très Physique*'. From having been a firebrand, she was relegated to the contemptible position of conventional wife. Their positions had begun to reverse. It was not in Violet's nature to be shy and retiring, despite her name. She wanted to be at the centre of things.

The Princesse de Polignac was able to supply exactly that – a background against which Violet could play the part of a rich, attractive Englishwoman whose past hinted at something just a little scandalous. The love affair with Vita Sackville-West was, of course, common knowledge to anyone who wished to find out, but time and distance, together with the more relaxed attitudes prevalent in Paris, served to put a gloss on the whole business, a gloss which only heightened Violet's reputation.

The princess was very different from beautiful, brooding, elusive Vita, and the way in which she treated Violet was indulgent. The princess had no interest whatsoever in setting the world on fire; her good reputation was far too valuable to her in the settled life she led. Of course people in the circles in which she moved knew exactly in which direction her tastes lay, but she preferred to keep her private life very private indeed. This suited Violet, who had learnt a hard lesson in the previous months about notoriety: she had discovered what social ruin was. Only two years earlier she had written in a pathetic letter to Pat Dansey:

Will you forgive me if I write you yet another afflicted letter? Please do, for I have no one to whom I can write openly except you. I do feel so *out* of everything, I am never asked to take part in the numerous expeditions, dinners, dances etc. that the others get up. I am always left out. I am always alone. I do feel it so. After all, it is a dreary sort of existence for anyone under thirty – I never have a friend to talk to. In Italy, there being no English people who *knew*, or at any rate, very few, it was so different.

Here they are barely civil. O Pat, I am one vast ache. . . . It is a hopeless position. My whole life seems ruined. I feel so maimed and bereft. I see only too clearly that it would be impossible for me to live in England. I cannot bear being snubbed and mortified. I am too proud. I prefer to live among people of a different class altogether, who would not look on me as a pariah and a déclassée. How black is my future! I can hardly bear to think of it . . .'.[6]

Mrs Keppel's spoilt little girl was not accustomed to such treatment; her relationship with the princess marked a changing point in her public behaviour. From now on, girlish enthusiasms and a desire to show the world, wild behaviour, and a complete disregard for wagging tongues, were put aside. Violet became a conformable creature, whose private behaviour might not bear close inspection but whose public image was above reproach: beautifully dressed, brilliantly witty, speaking her impeccable French, she was soon completely accepted into Parisian society.

For once, Violet was content. It was very flattering to be singled out for attention by such a person as the princess, and to be introduced to all the fascinating people she knew. And the princess knew everybody it seemed. Mrs Keppel was perfectly happy with the relationship, once it became obvious that she shared with the princess a common object: to avoid scandal at all costs. They were agreed on the obvious solution, for Violet to be closely chaperoned, either by her mother, or her husband.

Christmas 1923 saw the whole party on a Nile cruise aboard the princess's yacht. No doubt the trip included a visit to ancient Thebes where, in the spring of the year before, Howard Carter had discovered the tomb of Tutankhamun. It would have needed the combined presence of the princess and Mrs Keppel to get inside, however, since the intricate work of detailing the fabulous find was still in its first stages, and Howard Carter was determined to admit as few sightseers as possible. Most had to be content with sitting on the rubble outside, waiting for the occasional appearance of some priceless object being brought up to be packed to go to Cairo Museum. Aboard the princess's yacht everything had been meticulously arranged down to the last detail. Jacques Février, a good-looking young pianist, was one of the party and he helped to keep wilful Violet amused while Colonel and Mrs Keppel played bridge on deck with the princess. There were other trips too – to Greece, which was to Violet the inspiration she had always thought it might be.

'The Islands confirmed my suspicion that Beauty was the triumph of elimination, a lesson of self-denial, a strict diet to the mind. Temples reduced to two or three columns, continued to suggest entirety.'[7]

Violet's grandmother, Lady Edmonstone, was a daughter of the Governor of the Ionian Islands, and had been brought up in Ithaca. Violet felt her visit to Greece had put into perspective many of the qualities of her exquisite and much loved grandmother.

When they returned to France, Violet began to sit for her portrait by Jacques-Emile Blanche. She had first met him when she was a young girl, and he had come to have tea with her mother. Mrs Keppel had been called to court, and Violet had entertained the visitor instead, rather startling him with her grasp of Parisian slang. The portrait, painted when Violet was 32, shows an attractive young woman, seated, with her long slim legs crossed at the knee. She is fashionably dressed, and there is a slightly questioning look on her face as if she is gazing hopefully into the future. (The picture is now the property of the National Portrait Gallery.)

Meanwhile Denys was spending less time at his wife's side as the bank or insurance office where he worked had sent him to their branch at Brussels. From there he made in 1926 his second Russian trip, which, with a third trip in 1927, formed the inspiration of an unpublished manuscript *Stones of Emptiness* which he completed in 1928.

What sort of man was Denys Trefusis? None of his letters to Violet survives, and the only clues lie in the few remaining copies of the leather-bound volume. It is a fascinating document of the changes and existing conditions in 'that land of mystery and enchantment' ranging from descriptions of the landscape seen under the stars, to political discussion of the theories of communism and the economic disaster towards which he felt the U.S.S.R.

was heading. It is a well-organised, methodical piece of work from which its author emerges also as romantic, fastidious and sensitive.

His compassion was aroused by vast numbers of homeless child savages who roamed the streets, the result of the disparagement of parental authority and filial duty, and the suppression of all home life. Their ranks had been increased by thousands of illegitimate children, born because of the drop in moral standards. These children were worse off than animals, because they were not naturally equipped to fend for themselves.

'It is not easy to describe the appearance of these children. To say that they were clothed in rags means little in our usually hyperbolic speech. But their protection in all weathers generally consists of about two-thirds of a tattered coat, perhaps with only one sleeve or none, patched up in all sorts of incongruous ways, and about two thirds of a pair of trousers equally in tatters; the feet and head always bare. They are never washed. Their hair is never cut. Their filthiness is beyond description. But what is even more revolting is to see on those dirty little bodies, looking out from under a mass of filthy hair, faces that are full of savage cunning and of a dreadful experience. They slink about the streets with the sly, furtive look of wild animals in search of prey, and the only human touch about them seems to be their incessant cigarette-smoking. A large number of them are diseased, and it is appalling to realise that the most prevalent illness among them is venereal.'

He was a man with a sense of humour too. There are a number of anecdotes in the manuscript, such as the following:

'On the south side of the Krasnia Ploschchad stands one of the most astonishing churches I have ever seen, highly complicated in construction and profusely coloured like a gaudy sugar-cake, the church of St Basil. Its exterior is certainly one of the most hideous of all the works of man. It was severely damaged during the Bolshevik Revolution but has been well repaired, and the interior is now preserved as a museum. This church was built in the reign of Ivan the Terrible. The story goes that Ivan sent for an architect and ordered him to build the most beautiful church in Russia. When he saw the completed edifice he sent for the architect and asked him if he could build another similar church. "Oh yes, your Majesty, certainly", replied the delighted architect. "Well," said Ivan, "I'll take damned good care you don't," and forthwith had the wretched man's eyes put out.'

It is not clear exactly how the firm for which Denys worked had connections in Russia, though they obviously used him as their representative because he spoke fluent Russian. What exactly he was sent to achieve remains a mystery. But he obviously knew people in the country apart from business connections. A picture emerges of a quiet, thoughtful person who enjoyed a day's capercailzie shooting, ending in songs around the camp fire, a man who despite his poor health enjoyed outdoor life and appreciated natural beauty.

On his second trip in 1927, he was forced to leave in rather a hurry, though again, it is not completely clear why. He certainly appeared in court and was fined. His escape over the border by train, and his firm belief that he would be arrested at any moment, and brought back, makes exciting reading.

That same year, Violet and the Princesse de Polignac visited the United States of America, but their trip was not a success either.

'Though people were kindness itself, we quickly realised we were not for export. We were too lazy, too undemonstrative, too choosy, too introspective, too critical, above all, we were thickly encrusted with European barnacles, in a word, too old. We felt like a couple of misplaced adults in a rollicking nursery. We felt that we must get out before the monosyllable FLOP blazed in neon lights across our chests. We got out.'[8]

Cuba, where they went next, was a great deal more to Violet's taste. For a start, its sensual, primitive beauty struck an answering chord.

'The island had all the opulence of a Gobelins tapestry, crowded with fruit, conches, dolphins, palm trees. . . . Everything is voluptuous, beginning with the food, black *Moro* crabs with hooked claws like parrots' beaks, saffron-coloured rice used as a background for scarlet pimentos, green papoi with black seeds, small scented pink bananas.'[9]

After 1927 the intimate side of the relationship became less important, although Violet remained close friends with the princess until her death in London in 1943. Winnaretta had loved her very much but she became exasperated by Violet's childish desire to have her own way, and if the alliance of Mrs Keppel and the princess lent respectability to the affair, it also encouraged Violet to behave childishly. When there were two mother figures to indulge one childish one, the child could behave outrageously. As for Violet, it had been pleasant, but it was rather as if in Vita she had exchanged a galleon in full sail on the high seas in a thunderstorm for in Winnaretta a barge on a canal in quiet pastoral waters in the sunshine. Inside, the gypsy soul still craved excitement.

As a reaction against Vita, Winnaretta had meant a period of recovery, and reknitting of fibres, when the smashes and the vast emotional scars could be patched up. They might never completely disappear, but at least Violet was now firmly established in her new life, and ready to take with both hands all that Paris had to offer.

[6]
The green flame . . . hidden in the emerald

'She is very desirable I agree: very,' wrote Virginia to Vita about Violet on 14th June 1927. Virginia Woolf had been reading *Challenge*, Vita's book about the love affair, in which Violet was portrayed as the tempestuous Eve and she as Julian, torn between his loyalty for Athos (who represented Harold Nicolson) and his love for Eve. *Challenge* had been written between May 1918 and November 1919, at the height of their mutual passion, and many passages had been suggested and even written by Violet. Violet's own copy of the book is heavily marked in pencil. She often underscored passages and drew lines in the margins of her books to emphasise passages that had a particular significance for her, and *Challenge* is full of such marks.

Lady Sackville had managed to convince Vita that the book should be suppressed and it was not published in Britain until 1974, although it was published at the time in America by the George H. Doran Company. Violet's second portrayal in romantic literature was more subtle, and, fortunately, was not to meet a similar fate.

Virginia Woolf met Vita Sackville-West on 14th December 1922. Their friendship developed slowly for although Vita was enormously attracted by Virginia Woolf, Virginia regarded Vita with slight mistrust, so removed as she was in her élitist aristocratic world. Aloof and unembarrassed, she behaved in exactly the same fashion whatever the circumstances, whoever her companions. In July 1924, Virginia made her first visit to Knole and thought she understood Vita better as a result.

'You perambulate miles of galleries; skip endless treasures – chairs that Shakespeare might have sat on – tapestries, pictures, floors made of the halves of oaks; & penetrate at length to a round shiny table with a cover laid for one. A dozen glasses form a circle each with a red rose in it. What can one human being do to decorate itself in such a setting? One feels that one ought to be an elephant able to consume flocks & be hung about with whole blossoming trees – whereas one solitary peer sits lunching by himself in the centre, with his napkin folded into the shape of a lotus flower. Obviously, I did not keep my human values & my aesthetic values distinct. Knole is a conglomeration of buildings half as big as Cambridge I daresay; if you stuck Trinity Clare & King's together you might approximate. But the extremities & indeed the inward parts are gone dead. Ropes fence off half the rooms; the chairs & the pictures look preserved; life has left them. Not for a hundred years have the retainers sat down to dinner in the great hall. Then there is Mary Stuart's altar, where she prayed before her execution. "An ancestor of ours took her the death warrant" said Vita. All these ancestors & centuries, & silver & gold, have bred a perfect body. She is stag like, or race horse like, save for the face, which pouts, & has no very sharp brain. But as a body hers is perfection. So many rare & curious objects hit one's brain like pellets which perhaps may unfold later. . . . We motored down through Kent, which Vita loves, all very free & easy, supple jointed as the aristocrat is; no inhibitions, no false reserves; anything can be said; but as usual, that fatal simplicity or rigidity of mind which makes it seem all a little unshaded, & empty.'[1]

By the time *Orlando* was begun in 1927 both Vita and Knole had worked their magic. By the middle of October, Virginia was in full swing:

'I am writing at great speed. . . . The truth is I'm so engulfed in *Orlando* I can think of nothing else. . . . Tomorrow I begin the chapter which describes Violet and you meeting on the ice. The whole thing has got to be gone into thoroughly. I am swarming with ideas. Do give me some inkling of what sort of quarrels you had. Also, for what particular quality did she first choose you?'[2]

Orlando is a fantastic biographical novel, dedicated to Vita Sackville-West, in which the hero/heroine, Orlando, moves from Elizabethan to modern times, against the romantic background of an enormous country house, which is of course Knole. The book captures brilliantly the masculine/feminine appeal of Vita, drawing both men and women to her. Violet is portrayed as an immensely seductive Russian princess, Sasha, whose origins are slightly mysterious, and who encounters Orlando (then masculine) for the first time on the ice during a great Jacobean freeze of the Thames. She is a 'creature soft as snow, but with teeth of steel'. Although Orlando is betrothed to dull Lady Euphrosyne, he is immediately enraptured by the exotic, befurred vision from the Muscovite Embassy. At dinner, sitting opposite Orlando, she first turns to her neighbour and 'with a grace that ravished his heart' addresses him in her faultless French: "*La beauté des dames de la cour d'Angleterre me met dans le ravissement. On ne peut voir une dame plus gracieuse que votre reine, ni une coiffure plus belle que la sienne.*" Her neighbour is overcome with embarrassment since he speaks no French, and Sasha catches Orlando's eye across the table. He too speaks French with a perfect accent, and Sasha readdresses her question to him: 'Was that figure of fun at the end of the table with her hair rigged up like a Maypole (*comme une grande perche mal fagotée*) really the Queen?'

This is the start of a tempestuous love affair which is to end in elopement but although Orlando waits for hours at the appointed place, Sasha does not appear, and in the breaking dawn, he sees the black flags atop the tall masts of the Russian ships far out to sea from the Thames estuary, and knows his love has flown.

The book was published in 1928 and was a great success. Vita was delighted with it. Violet's reaction is unrecorded but it is superficially a flattering portrayal, after all. She is depicted as an irresistible creature, beautiful and bizarre. 'Extraordinary seductiveness . . . issued from the whole person.'

The clues are all there: 'eyes which looked as if they had been fished from the bottom of the sea'; 'she talked so enchantingly, so wittily, so wisely, (but unfortunately always in French).'

Yet with all this there is an uneasy undercurrent of wantonness, recklessness, not stressed but there for anyone who cared to look. Violet was well known for the sort of behaviour that Princess Sasha indulges in at the banquet. Prepared to be outwardly polite in company, in private she could have a wicked tongue, and not even her best friends were spared when she cared to make jokes at their expense. At one point in the description of Orlando's infatuation for his princess, they return to the Russian ship so Sasha may collect some clothes from a chest. She seems to be taking an unconscionably long time. Orlando goes to investigate. By the sudden flare of a flickering flame, he thinks he sees his ice princess in the hot embrace of a swarthy sailor. He is unwilling to believe the evidence of his own eyes, but another unattractive image springs to his mind: Sasha gnawing a wax candle, like a rat. There is a hint, the merest suggestion, of something unpleasant.

For all that Virginia Woolf expressed it: 'in all she said, however open she seemed and voluptuous, there was something hidden; in all she did however daring, there was something concealed. So the green flame is hidden in the emerald . . .', the compliment, for those who cared to burrow under the pearls and sables, was rather dubious. There is something not quite right about her, something the reader is left to guess at, something so understated and undefined that it is more effectively conveyed than if it had been expressly described. It leaves a sour taste in the mouth.

Another book published in 1928 Violet probably read with interest was *The Well of Loneliness* by Radclyffe Hall. Marguerite Radclyffe Hall was a notorious lesbian who had, after a troubled search for the right person, settled down with Una Troubridge. Radclyffe Hall is notorious because Una Troubridge's husband, Sir John Troubridge, had objected to his wife's desertion to another woman, and had cited Radclyffe Hall as co-respondent, in a blaze of publicity. It would be scandalous enough now, when such things are accepted as a matter of course; needless to say, people were simply horrified at the time.

The Well of Loneliness is a novel about sexual inversion. Its heroine, Stephen Gordon, is, like her creator, a lesbian, a woman searching for a settled life with a kindred spirit. It is a convincing and compassionate book, just as readable now as it was then. When it appeared in 1928, it was almost immediately suppressed. A review in the *Sunday Times* said: 'I would rather give a healthy boy or a healthy girl a phial of prussic acid than this novel.'

It was available in Paris, however, and probably Violet read a copy of it there.

Thus, liaisons between women were in the news at the end of the 1920s. Paris had a well-known lesbian clique, some of whose members had been sympathetically portrayed in *The Well of Loneliness*. If she had wanted to pursue these particular tastes, Violet would have had no lack of opportunity. Apart from her own personal attractions, she had the undoubted enhancement of Vita and Winnaretta in her past. But the firebrand who had so outrageously flaunted the hypocritical rules laid down by her mother's generation had changed. There would always, like Sasha, be 'something concealed', a past which would always be associated with her, a mysterious quality to her reputation, but outwardly conformity had won the day.

It was now that Violet finished and had published her first novel, *Sortie de secours*, 'a mediocre little book, a patchwork affair, aphorisms, maxims, annotations, loosely woven into the shape of a novel. It served its purpose, it was a loophole, an outlet, above all, a piece of blotting paper which absorbed my obsessions.'[3] The book was also a vehicle for her views on various countries and cities.

Sortie de secours is the only one of Violet Trefusis's novels which goes deeply into the thoughts and feelings of its heroine, and is less polished as a result. Later Violet wrote, '*J'écris avec mon cerveau et non pas avec mon coeur,*' but in *Sortie de secours* this is not really true: the veneer of sophistication is transparent enough to see through to the heart of the writer. Significantly, it is written in the first person and the heroine, Laure, a widow for two years living in a beautiful house at Auteuil has more in common with her author than mere circumstances. When Violet called her book an 'outlet', she spoke truly, for the book holds all the signs of someone who is undergoing a purge. In the early chapters, the squabbles between Laure and Drino are surely echoes of those Violet had with Denys. His growing indifference and teasing detachment serve only to make her more dependent, more clinging. In order to make him love her more, Laure decides to leave Paris and hopes he will miss her in her absence. All goes according to plan until Laure encounters Oradour, a painter, whom she had met briefly once in Paris. It is certainly not in her plans that she should fall in love with him, but this is what happens. She returns to Paris to try to sort herself out, decides that her love for Oradour is the most important thing in the world, and races back to Avignon to see him. Something which happens on the train reverses her decision, and in the end she decides what really matters is independence and resolves to take the emergency exit into the great unknown.

'In every person there is an emergency exit; a self-interest which in its various expressions allows one to escape when an obsession becomes too violent, and to disappear with a mocking laugh. The disadvantage is that one cannot always come back. . . .'[4]

There are echoes, too, of the women who had loved so much Vita Sackville-West. The ache of the broken heart is only too obvious and the resigned acceptance of becoming a different sort of person. 'I am forced to admit that I do not have any of the good or bad qualities which make love flourish. Happiness comes to me from things, not people.'[5]

This was the beginning of a writing career which ended only with her death, and the publication posthumously of *From dusk to dawn*. Unfortunately, it was a career which was to be spasmodic and intermittent. There is no doubt that Violet Trefusis had immense talent, but she did not work hard at it. Like Eve, in *Challenge*, she did not take her talents as seriously as some other writers took theirs.

'You are too richly gifted, Eve, to abandon yourself to such slackness of life.''

'"I told you, I had no strength of character," she said with bitterness, "what are my gifts, such as they are to me?"'

Had she had the relentless drive of some writers who have to live by their writing, she might have become a writer of even greater distinction. As it was, she dabbled, with charm and wit, but dabbled nonetheless, not using her gifts to the maximum, producing book after book – four in French, five in English – but all running to the same format. As lightweight reading, they are perfect of their kind: witty and clever and extremely well-written. They concern smart people living in grand houses. Violet's heroes and heroines are the sort of people who sat down at her dining-room table.

That so much talent could not have produced even better books is very sad. But the young girl who wrote such beautiful, glowing letters was a very different creature from the woman Violet was becoming: afraid to be serious, to trust her emotions. After *Sortie de secours*, her writing is on a purely superficial level; it would be in the worst of bad taste for her to reveal too much. But the talent is all there, like a hard sheen of brilliant lacquer. There is little doubt that Violet Trefusis could have written some really worthwhile books had she been able to bring to bear the sort of discipline that every writer needs. Had she, like Virginia Woolf, or even Vita, been able to make herself sit down at a particular time for a specific period, or until a certain number of pages had been written, she might have acquired the habit of sustained effort. But Violet hated a humdrum, regular life. Never in a million years would she have been content at Sissinghurst, writing and gardening. One of the facets of her charm was a craving for excitement, a catalystic quality of making dramas happen. She could be devastatingly amusing, and she liked to be amused. The current love affair, entertaining, the social round and – most disastrous of all – a loathing of being on her own, were all parts of a life which led to a lack of proper concentration on her writing. There is no doubt she had the highest ability, and lacked only application. She did not even have the incentive of the need to earn her living.

Strangely enough, the actual need to do this was something Denys Trefusis considered important and as long ago as his pamphlet entitled *A Short Essay upon Moral Retrogression under Socialism* had written:

'There is another point, and this chiefly with regard to music, to which I personally attach no little importance. It is an undeniable fact that many of the best and greatest works of musical art we possess have been produced under conditions of poverty, and, in some cases, of extreme poverty. Very few of the world's greatest musicians have been anything but poor men, and, with the sole exception of Mendelssohn, they have none of them been wealthy. And it must be said that Mendelssohn, who was one of the greatest geniuses that have ever lived, might have written finer music than he did, had he been compelled to write for his living. It appears that the production of great musical work needs the stimulus of poverty.'

Shortly after *Sortie de secours* was published, Denys, whose health had been poor for many years, died at the American Hospital at Neuilly. He had been seriously ill the year before and had gone to stay in Buckinghamshire with his sister Elizabeth, who had always been devoted to him. Her daughter, Naomi, vividly recalls him, charming and debonair, in his pyjamas, working in the garden on the manuscript of *Stones of Emptiness*, surrounded by books and with papers constantly blown away by the wind. But at night she would hear him shouting in his sleep; he was mentally as well as physically ill.

At the end of the year he was well enough to return to Paris, but in the summer word reached his sister that the old chest infection had flared up again and that he was at a convent hospital. She and Denys's brother Kerr went straight to France and had him moved to the American Hospital where he died on 2nd September 1929.

Throughout most of his illness, Denys was looked after by a young Australian nurse who became very devoted to him. Until 1976, she wrote annually to Elizabeth, on the anniversary of Denys's death.

Violet was conspicuous by her absence from the sick room however. She never could bear illness or hospitals and the sight of his suffering was too much. Occasionally she did come, and putting her beautifully coiffed head round the door to his room, enquired if he would like a little '*mousse de jambon*' or some other delicacy. But her real instinct was to run away.

In the end, whatever their relations had been, whatever cruelties on a large scale Violet had inflicted on Denys, whatever indifferences on a small scale Denys had inflicted on Violet, there is no doubt she sincerely mourned him.

'I have known many remarkable men, I have never known a braver, a more prodigal. He had all the ballad-like qualities I most admire, I, all the defects it was most difficult for him to condone. Nevertheless, there was a great link between us, we both loved poetry, France, travel, being insatiably interested in foreign countries. We were both Europeans in the fullest sense of the term.

The same things made us laugh, we quarrelled a lot, loved not a little. We were more to be envied than pitied.'[6]

This unlikely marriage had begun in extraordinary circumstances and had weathered many storms. Denys Trefusis had not spent much time at his wife's side after she met the Princesse de Polignac, and during that relationship, Violet had learned to stand on her own feet and had learned to do without him. She had made a circle of friends, written a book, and become a figure in Parisian society.

In 1931, *Echo*, Violet's second book in French was published. This was a novel about Scotland, Scotland for the French, that is. The action takes place in a bleak Scottish baronial house surrounded by brooding moors. Lady Balquidder and her twin nephew and niece, Malcolm and Jean Macfinnish, await the arrival, not without misgiving, of the twins' glamorous French cousin, Sauge de Cervallon, who has been ill, and thought to need a six-week holiday in a remote region far from the exigencies of her demanding life in Paris, and her husband, Alain. The twins are completely identical and completely inseparable and resent the intrusion of the foreigner, but predictably enough, the charm of the Parisian soon begins to work on them, and before long, both are madly in love with her. For a time, Sauge imagines that she is in love with Malcolm, but a letter from her husband brings her to her senses. She goes to break the news that she is leaving Glendrocket to Malcolm, he takes her in his arms and is covering her with kisses, when Jean comes in. Heartbroken, Jean rushes out into the wild Scottish night, and her dead body is recovered later. Malcolm turns on Sauge, ordering her to go, and never return.

It is a highly atmospheric book, a series of occurrences which give rise to an eerie, uneasy feeling, culminating in the tragedy at the end.

There are signs that the voluntary exile still missed her native land. Sauge writes to Alain en route from Dover to London, in the train.

'We are skirting a park which harbours in its heart a vast redbrick residence which must date from the time of Elizabeth I and reminds me of all that I love about England; its tranquillity, its good manners, its humour, its grocery shops where they sell caviar along with crepe-soled shoes, its Queen Anne architecture, its birds, its ghosts. . . .

'I love its country life with its starched housemaids and its bath salts.'[7]

The descriptions of the Scottish scene are lifted straight from memories of childhood holidays at Duntreath, the Brackens in *Echo* changed only in name from the real-life lodgekeeper and his wife, the Strachans. Even some local neighbours, the Campbells, appear without even a changed name to protect their identity.

Just as Violet Trefusis enjoyed showing her view of France to the English, she is showing her view of Scotland to the French. It is an affectionate representation, amused and aware, with perhaps a tribute to her Scottish mama.

'Scotswomen are the most level-headed in the world, but they will say to you with total unconcern:

'"As I was going to bed yesterday evening, I saw the knight's head on the dressing-table, that's three times in two months – would you kindly pass the salt."'[8]

Echo was a much more polished book than *Sortie de secours* and made a name for Violet in Paris. The book sold well; it was even nominated for the Prix Fémina.

Next came *Broderie anglaise* which was published in France in 1935 and is perhaps her most accomplished novel in French.

Set in Oxford, the book is about a successful writer, Alexa Harrowby Quince, who for five years has been involved with Lord Shorne, completely dominated by his unpleasant mother. It is a book about the power of the absent influence.

Alexa meets John Shorne immediately after his romance with his cousin, Anne Lindell, has collapsed and Anne has departed to France, where she has married someone else. For five years, Alexa has lived with the shadow of Anne between them, the sensuous, vital, vivid woman *'faite à ravir'* that John has evoked for her, and with whom she can never compete.

Then one afternoon, a mutual friend brings Anne, who is also a writer, to tea with Alexa, and after some initial skirmishes, the two women discuss John Shorne, and the truth of the love affair between John and Anne is revealed. Far from being Anne who abandoned John, it was John who, at the insistence of his sinister mother, abandoned Anne, the night before the wedding. John is exposed to Alexa in a strong light: a weak deceiver, false to his ideals. And yet, ultimately, all is not lost. Anne's visit has put an end to the old love Alexa once had for John, but that love was excessive.

'I loved you too much and you did not love me enough. I did not know how to "play the game"; she has shown me how. She has taught me more things in one hour than I had learnt in the whole of my life. She is a pacemaker, an experienced and sensual person, experienced in sensuality.'[9]

It is a sensual book: Anne's femininity is immediately established by her description. '"*Sa bouche? Une fraise boudeuse.*"' There is a fantastic *scène de séduction* reminiscent of Vita Sackville-West's in *The Edwardians* when John leads Alexa through the vast richly decorated saloons of his ancestral home to the Charles II room where the deed is accomplished. The room closely resembles the King's Bedroom at Knole with its solid and florid silver furniture. There is an evocative description of an old-fashioned English tea:

'The drawing room smelt of bread and butter, tea and the shy scent of jonquils. Alexa put some coal back on the fire and resumed her inspection of the tea-table. Entering unknowingly, a stranger would have seen a meal fit for children. It was scarcely believable that a grown-up person would spoil his digestion by eating so many sugary things. Fancy biscuits of an improbable pink were snuggled against pyramids of cream puffs; a chocolate cake dribbled jam. In the crannies of the rock cakes glittered flints of sugar. Not to speak of the jars of jam, or of the honeycomb which had burst its wooden corset and which was spreading out in a golden flood.

'In the middle of this sparkling company, the eclairs, swarthy and glum, were lined up close together like a disagreeable family which would not have been introduced . . .'.[10]

But out of the ashes of her dead love, Alexa finds a balanced formula for her love and life. In a different way, she still loves John and she can fit this love into her life-style. The book ends on a note of hope . . . but the heady scent of the departed Anne lingers in the air.

Violet's last novel in French, *Les Causes perdues*, followed in 1941. This novel concerns various people living or connected with a small town near Poitiers, each of whom has his or her own pet 'lost cause'. There is rich Madame de Béanthes, starving and freezing herself to death in the lost cause of her nephew, Ghislain, interested only in his boyfriends and his inheritance of her money. He cannot even wait for her to be completely dead before pulling the ruby ring from her little finger. There is Madame de Petitpas and her brother, Emmanuel, whose lost cause is Marie-Charlotte, *jeune fille pro-longée*, though not strictly old maid. Her life is one of drudgery and service to others, but Emmanuel leaving his fortune to her makes no difference. It is too late to change. Marie-Charlotte's lost cause is her chauffeur, Mégot, with whom she is guiltily and hopelessly in love. He ends by murdering a helpless old lady. But as Marie-Charlotte says:

'I feel terribly dull in the middle of these assertive personalities each of whom knew how to create a style: this does not mean that they are particularly happy, but perhaps happiness does not interest them . . .'.[11]

Happiness is definitely an aspiration of the bourgeoisie; grand people think it is far more chic to be miserable.

Violet's novels in English involve the same sort of people involved in the same kind of plots. In fact, most of the action takes place both in England and France, or England and Italy, so that she is able to compare and contrast the two countries, a talent she uses to the full, sometimes to the disadvantage of her native country.

Tandem, published in 1933, is about two Greek sisters, one of whom takes Paris by storm and marries a French duke, and the other of whom marries an Englishman with a large country house, modelled on Berkeley Castle. The mother of the French duke is supposed to be a caricature of Anna de Noailles and there is more than a suggestion of Mrs Arthur James, that well-known Edwardian renowned for her astounding carefulness with money, in the character of Madame de Megrondes. Violet's friend, Pat Dansey, appears in the guise of Nancy, as does her uncle, Lord Fitzhardinge, thinly disguised as Lord Destry, even down to the Persian cats entwined about his person, and through whom he addresses his occasional remarks.

Reading Violet's autobiography, *Don't Look Round*, which she was to write in her sixties, one is struck by the frequent direct quotations from *Tandem*: descriptive passages, characters, places, all indiscriminately used again, but sometimes with the thin veiling removed. It is rather unsettling that the excellent description of Gervase in *Tandem* is more or less exactly used again to describe Denys Trefusis, in *Don't Look Round*, even down to the ruff and one pearl earring. Probably *Tandem* was not much read by the early 1950s, and Violet thought she could lift some of the better passages without anyone being any the wiser. It certainly detracts from both books. There is one passage, describing the influence of art nouveau, which was to appear twice more, once in *Don't Look Round* and again in *Memoirs of an Armchair* in practically identical form.

Apart from this, there are some amusing moments in *Tandem*:

'Summer the secure had vanished, and in her place was a gipsy dressed in tatters, wild and wanton: shots pricked the crisp air; out of the wood bordering the park pheasants came hurrying in fatal finery, like gaudy courtiers surprised by revolution. One thought: If only they had time to change into something less conspicuous!'

And some revealing ones:

'She adored all the paraphernalia, the frills and furbelows of love, she enjoyed posing as a *grande amoureuse*, but though sensuous, she was not sensual, and she was quite content to remain in love's antechamber.'

Except for those who have a taste for such period pieces, the book is rather heavy going now. It is so much of its time that it makes strange reading. Fashionable, frivolous and faded is *Tandem*; with relief one turns to *Hunt the Slipper*, published in 1937. It was also published in France in 1938 under the title *Il Court, Il Court*, translated by Jean Talva, who had translated the works of Rosamund Lehmann.

Here is a real story, dated perhaps, but something a reader can get his teeth into, characters about whom he might be inspired to care, and whose fates and dilemmas are of some interest to him. It has a highly amusing plot with a neat twist at the end, and Violet is at her very best describing the games people play.

'He was pleasantly surprised at her unpunctuality: was her technique improving at last? He glanced at his wristwatch. A quarter of an hour late: in another ten minutes he would be in love with her.'

Nigel Benson (*la savate* of the title?) half-French, half-English, and nearing a sensitive middle-age falls in love with Caroline Crome, the wife of his neighbour Sir Anthony Crome, during a visit to Paris. They meet by chance in a nightclub, where Caroline is dancing with a handsome Chilean, Melo Gabilla ('"Do you know Melo Gabilla?" Nigel felt he should know Melo Gabilla, that without him his education was incomplete') – with whom she is passionately in love. Unfortunately, 'fashion rather than passion' dictates Melo's affairs, and he is soon lured away by the dazzling Terpsichore van Pusch. This leaves the field open for Nigel, first in the role of comforter and chief support, and later as lover, but in the end he misses the mark, and the affair ends in heartbreak for both of them, but not, one cannot help thinking, without a tiny feeling of relief on the part of Nigel.

The title of the book sums it all up: 'Love passed from one to the other, furtive, unseizable, like the slipper in "Hunt the Slipper"'. The person you love always loves someone else better, and you always love someone better than the person who loves you.

It is a highly sophisticated and polished book, an amusing and detached study of love and its attendant rituals, written by a woman who knows full well what it is to love, to suffer, and to be philosophical about it afterwards, even eventually to laugh at her own expense.

[7]
La Tour Prends Garde

Writing was one distraction, travelling another. The travel bug had bitten Violet early, with visits to Biarritz and Paris, to Italy and Spain, the long trip to Ceylon and the time in Munich. Now she had been to America and Cuba with Winnaretta de Polignac, on a Nile cruise, to the Greek islands, to Vienna and Berlin.

But roots were becoming important too. In 1927 Violet acquired a medieval tower in the country, eighty kilometres from Paris on the road to Provins. The events leading up to this were worthy of the strange atmosphere of the house itself.

Violet met Marcel Proust at a luncheon given by Walter Berry, the friend of Edith Wharton. As far as Proust himself was concerned, the meeting was a disappointment, for Proust was self-absorbed in his failing health. But he did manage to exert himself enough to tell her about a village called St Loup de Naud, the name he had used in his Swann books. Proust told Violet she should try to find it.

Some years afterwards, on looking through a copy of *A la Recherche du temps perdu*, the name of St Loup recalled the conversation to Violet and on a sudden whim, she set out in search of St Loup de Naud. In a distinctly Proustian vein, she describes in *Don't Look Round* how she was immediately captivated by the village and the tower that rose romantically from a sea of trees from behind the Romanesque church tower. The tower in the trees was to become, with additions, her country house.

There was a special atmosphere at St Loup, the extravagant and grotesque combined, which exactly suited Violet and provided the sort of stage setting against which she could enact all kinds of strange fantasies. The property had once been the site of a

The tower at Saint-Loup, photo by Stanislas Lamarche

Violet, portrait by Jacques-Emile Blanche, 1926

monastery and there was still a trace of a contemplative atmosphere which some thought spooky. Many were the ghost stories told by visitors to St Loup.

Denys Trefusis had created a formal garden, which he loved. From a round pool in the centre, he created alleyways in all directions, edged with small box hedges. Some of the hedges were allowed to grow, and on these he practised topiary.

By this time, Violet was a confident and accomplished hostess, justifiably famous for the excellence of her table. St Loup was near enough to Paris to make it an ideal place for weekend parties. The comfort and company to be found there, as well as its unique atmosphere, made it a popular place to be asked to. Violet describes its special appeal:

'I'm afraid the character of St Loup cannot be described as "nice". It is sensuous, greedy as a Venetian courtesan, with the same insatiable taste for velvets the colour of rotten peaches. It is ruthless, vindictive, capricious. If it takes a dislike to you, you are done. A pipe bursts in your room before you have been there five minutes. You fall, twisting your ankle badly, down the corkscrew stairs, the fire in the bedroom smokes to such an extent that you are reminded of the last act of the Valkyries. If, on the other hand, you have the good fortune to please St Loup, it is equally unscrupulous. No *scène de séduction* is too crude, no posture too audacious. It beckons, importunes, detains.

'It has been called by many names. La Tour Prends Garde, Le Chequers français, La Melisandière. Yet the soul of St Loup is rugged and unfathomable. It is not duped by its recreations.'[1]

In the years between the buying of St Loup in 1927 and the outbreak of war, Violet entertained lavishly there. Inside she made the house dramatically beautiful and she was becoming an expert at arranging parties so that her guests were both entertained and entertaining.

She still had her flat in Paris and had an established circle of friends. But she was not happy. She was rich, she was bored, and she was lonely. There was nothing in her life that consumed her in the way that loving Vita had. The various parts of her life, her houses, entertaining, her social life, her writing, her mother, none of these alone or combined occupied her mind and heart. It was as well that she did not know that there was never to be another Vita, for she knew that trivial love affairs were no substitute for the all-absorbing passion she had once known. 'I was unfortunately not one of those women who replace love by little love affairs.'[2]

Virginia Woolf had taken the place of Violet in Vita's heart but no-one, male or female, ever really touched Violet's heart deeply. The armour had come down and no arrows could penetrate its fastness.

Soon after Denys's death, Violet received a surprise proposal from a very unlikely suitor, Max Jacob. Some twenty years older than Violet, Max Jacob had lived most of his adult life in Paris and was friendly with Picasso and André Salmon. Apart from painting, he also wrote poetry, and was renowned as a wit and a dandy. But there was a deeply religious side to him; in his forties he was converted to catholicism and went into retreat for six years. In 1927 he came back to Paris and temporarily resumed his old life of frivolity, when presumably the marriage proposal was made.

'(He) called on me one afternoon, dressed, he imagined, for the part of a suitor. A small dapper Pulchinello, he wore a top hat, white spats, gloves the colour of fresh butter. He hung his hat on his stick which he held like a banner between his legs. He was irresistible. I longed to take advantage of his proposal which was couched in terms that sounded as though he had learned them out of a book on etiquette. We examined the pros and cons. St Loup, far from being an asset, proved a stumbling block.

'"*Je déteste la campagne*", said Max, "*tout y est trop vrai!* The nearest I ever get is the Bois, and that is bad enough, because it *reminds* me of the country."

'"What about travel?"

'"That is different, the place doesn't belong to me, there are no responsibilities. *C'est comme je mangeais au restaurant.*"

'A great advantage, he pointed out, was his being about twenty years older than me. "I have waited forty years before proposing to anyone. I am not likely to propose to anyone else."'[3]

Nor, it seems, did he, for he returned to the religious institution of Saint-Benoit and devoted the rest of his life there to meditation

Max Jacob, drawing by Modigliani

and prayer. In 1944, he was arrested by the Germans and sent to a concentration camp at Drancy, where he died soon afterwards of consumption. His courage and loving kindness in the camp was an example and an inspiration to his fellow prisoners.

There were other proposals: some were made and turned down, others made and nothing came of them. Still more were simply jokes. Diana Mosley tells a story in her autobiography about dining with Violet in Paris on the way back from Rome, in company with Lord Berners.

'When we got to Paris we dined with Violet Trefusis. She said to Gerald how amusing it would be for them to pretend to be engaged and get a deluge of presents. A day or two later we were all back in London and their forthcoming engagement was announced in the gossip column of a newspaper. Violet telephoned Gerald: "I've had dozens of telegrams of congratulations".

'"Have you really?" said Gerald, "I haven't had a single one!"'

'Her mother, Mrs Keppel, who happened to be in London, thought the joke had gone too far and issued a denial. Gerald said he was going to put in the *Times* "Lord Berners has left Lesbos for the Isle of Man".'[4]

A more eligible *parti* was Comte Stanislas de la Rochefoucauld, eligible except that he had no money, was a crashing bore, and was still married to the actress, Alice Cocéa. Mrs Keppel dealt with him too, in her own inimitable fashion, musing aloud how it was not her intention to give Violet a second dowry and how much of her first there might still be left. 'Violet is *such* a child!' The count's attentions immediately began to dwindle. Violet got her own back some time later when, after his divorce from Alice Cocéa, and his marriage to a woman from their own set, Yvonne, he observed at a lunch party one day, 'It's extraordinary, but when I married Alice, a lot of people thought I would become an actor.' 'And now dear Stanislaus,' retorted Violet sweetly, 'now that you've married a lady, do people expect you to become a gentleman?'

Violet was seriously involved for a time with Paul Reynaud, whom she met first at a luncheon party at Vichy, forgot, and then several years later at another luncheon given by Gaston Palewski, Reynaud's secretary. Violet had greatly admired his work as

Minister of Finance, and after the lunch, began to see a great deal of him. He was already ruled by two women: his wife, and Comtesse Hélène de Portes, but this in no way deterred Violet, inspired no doubt by nostalgia for the days when her mother had held the hand that ruled a large part of the world. For a time, Violet saw herself in the role of political hostess, an indispensible intermediary between a grateful nation and an enraptured future prime minister. Once more the fantasy probably far outshone the reality, although the liaison was not so unlikely as perhaps it might initially appear. In many ways an Anglophile, Paul Reynaud was fascinated by an Englishwoman so completely integrated into France. Violet was fascinated by his brilliant technique in the Chambre, a tough political creature who knew the works of Du Bellay by heart. Politics and poetry were an unusual combination, the appeal of the intellectual and the romantic.

A more light-hearted interlude occupied Violet's heart in the winter of 1930. Emotionally prepared by the beautiful stark countryside of Central Europe, the bitter cold of the climate and the gypsy romance of Budapest, Violet could not but succumb.

'The Hungarians, how good looking! They would be photographed standing behind rows of game, pheasants, hares, partridges, stags, wild boars. Game. That's what they were: game for anything.'[5]

Particularly persistent in search of fair game was the Regent's son, Estvan Horthy. Tall and handsome, magnificently glamorous in his uniform, Estvan Horthy was supposed to be laying siege to an Italian princess. Instead, he rented a house in Budapest and acquired a sledge complete with musicians, on which he whisked Violet away to nightclubs. Cheek to cheek, they danced the nights away to the strains of gypsy violins, while the stars glittered diamond bright over the frozen landscape and the Danube rushed by, impetuous as the dancers themselves.

Two of Violet's friends who came to stay were not so enthusiastic, however. Violet recorded their reaction and her own less starry-eyed summary of her feelings towards Hungary in an article some years later.

'They thought the architecture hideous, the food indigestible,

Paul Reynaud,
surrounded by his Cabinet

Estvan Horthy,
vice-regent of Hungary

the restaurants expensive, the gypsies superfluous, the Hungarians half-witted. I saw their point. Only one half of me responded to all this, certainly not the more fastidious half. I can still hear one of my French friends muttering: *"Je boude à Bude, je peste contre Pest"*. It was an experience not to be repeated.

'If you pin me down as to why I was fond of Budapest, I will reply that I liked it because I have: (a) a cult for cold, properly organised, (b) I love Second Empire architecture, Hungarian version, (c) I find incomprehensible languages intoxicating. In short, I am a middle-Europe fan. It is a wonderful holiday of the intellect.'[6]

Paris, in the years leading up to the Second World War, was full of fascinating people, some of whom are described in *Don't Look Round*. There was Anna de Noailles whom Violet met at the salon of the Princesse de Polignac. One wonders how flattered the countess would have been by the brilliant description of herself in *Don't Look Round*, although no doubt she preferred it to Edith Sitwell's description – 'the old girl who writes bad poetry'!

In an unpublished piece among her private papers, Violet wrote some years later:

'Much has yet to be written about the group of Eastern European *femmes savantes*, exotic, neurotic, despotic, who dominated Parisian society in the twenties. The most beautiful was Marthe Bibesco, the novelist, the most gifted, Anna de Noailles, the poet. Half Roumanian, half Greek, self-styled gavroche, de Byzance acclaimed her as a genius adulated as a woman, this tiny tropical creature imposed her caprices even as Cleopatra forced her whims on Anthony. The Bibliothèque Nationale has just organised an exhibition of her works. Tributes from the pen of Rilke, Proust, Barrès, and d'Annunzio, are here assembled. Anna's beautiful arched and prancing handwriting, compared by Proust to branches of honeysuckle, is a smaller edition of d'Annunzio's more preposterous one (might not both be derived from Ronsard's. . . ?) Madame de Noailles' pastel portraits of contemporaries, explosive, impatient, enliven the walls. She rushed in where angels fear to tread, scattering experience and theories right and left. She knew everything by intuition; once wrote a scholarly essay on Spain which she had only glimpsed from a train window.'

Jean Cocteau's reaction corresponded to Violet's: neither was the least taken in by the act Anna de Noailles put on, but neither could help being impressed by it. Scattering scarves, beads, bracelets, hairpins and other varieties of her adornment, this minute woman captivated her audience, simply by talking.

'She sniffed, sneezed, burst out laughing, heaved heart-rending sighs and dropped Turkish necklaces and scarves. Then she took a deep breath and, curling and uncurling her lips at full speed, she began. What did she say? I no longer know. I know that she talked and talked and talked and the big room filled with a crowd of people and the young ones sat on the floor and the older ones sat in armchairs. I know that the Princesse de Polignac and the Princesse de Caraman-Chimay (her friend and her sister) standing on her left and her right, seemed to be seconds in some dreamland boxing-ring. I know that the servants in their black suits and the footmen in knee-breeches and powdered wigs came closer to the half-open doors. I know that through the open windows of June, like the waltz in a film by Lubitsch or in that film where Liszt played the piano, the words of the Comtesse bewitched the trees, the plants and the stars – that her words penetrated into the neighbouring buildings, interrupted quarrels, enriched sleep, and that everything and everyone, from the star to the tree, from the tree to the chauffeurs of the waiting limousines, murmured "The Comtesse is talking . . . the Comtesse is talking . . . the Comtesse is talking . . ."'.[7]

The beautiful Princesse Marthe Bibesco was, like her cousin, Anna de Noailles, half Roumanian. 'Naturally' wrote Violet in *Prelude to Misadventure*, 'they detested each other. Queen Elizabeth and Mary Stuart did not plot one another's undoing with more zest than these two'.

A frequent visitor to the enormous palace near Bucharest owned by the princess was King Carol of Roumania, a very close friend.

'Ondine-like, (the palace) . . . rose from the lake, it rose from a carpet of iris and water lily. A seventeenth century Venetian architect had built it in the Lombard style. Like the Doge's Palace, it was the colour of a tired gardenia, or, if you prefer, a kid glove, the day after the ball. It looked both worn and festive.

Princesse Marthe Bibesco, 1925

Inside, the floors were made of gold mosaic, there were grilles and leopard skins, thrones and divans, a peacock preened itself on the marble steps . . .'.[8]

No less exotic was its owner, '*inlassable Schéhérézade*', chewing pensively on a tuberose, wrapped in sables, or dripping with emeralds.

The friendship of the two writers was a long-lasting one, cemented by Violet who dedicated *Hunt the Slipper* to the princess. In the princess's book, *Au Jardin de Marcel Proust*, she wrote:

'*A Violet Trefusis, Royaliste, romantique, romancière et personnage de roman qui a choisi Saint Loup pour résidence, Florence pour capitale et Paris pour passer le temps, cette invitation de faire ensemble une promenade sentimentale,*

'*son amie Marthe Bibesco.*'

Very different was Colette, whom Violet, to her surprise, found to be cosy, more interested in the making of salad dressing and water divining, the choosing of a cheese in a perfect state of ripeness, the correct categorisation of a plant, than in playing the role of a famous woman of letters. Although she had lived in Paris for many years, Colette had never lost her deep childhood love for the country, a love that was compounded by her devotion to her mother. Despite her success as a writer and her following in literary circles, she remained in many ways unsophisticated and certainly never aimed at being smart or fashionable. But Violet admired her work: in the art of describing the theme of love, 'she is a virtuoso, playing on our heart strings with the fearful familiarity of a Kreisler'.[9]

It was Colette who, meeting Violet for the first time, exclaimed, 'Violette? Ah non, plutôt Géranium!'

The most notorious of the members of the select lesbian set was perhaps Nathalie Clifford Barney, 'the wild girl from Cincinnati' as she was known, a rich American who lived in rue Jacob where she held regular receptions on Fridays. All kinds of people were to be found at rue Jacob that day: Romaine Brooks, another rich American and her most constant companion, might be there, and the large squat figure of Gertrude Stein. 'A pose is a pose is a pose', said Violet dismissively after an encounter in a bookshop.

Violet preferred grander people, and had no inclination whatsoever to move in such a circle where her past might have won her special favours. She was determined to become as French as the French and to be absorbed into the sort of life she had known in England before the war, the life of the élite in an exclusive set. She knew the rules and she knew where she stood.

A particularly special friend in these circles was Antoinette d'Harcourt, the first wife of the Duc d'Harcourt. Violet lived in part of their house for a time. She and the duchess shared literary interests, though the duchess's talents lay in writing poetry. Indeed, Eluard considered her to be the greatest French poet alive.

In 1924, the Keppels had bought from a Russian countess a villa high on the hill of Bellosguardo in Florence. It was called Villa dell'Ombrellino and had for a short time been the home of Galileo. Architecturally of not much interest, the house had two magnificent views, each enhanced by the contrast it presented to the other. One side looked out, over numerous statues, to the rolling landscape of Tuscany, unchanged for centuries, punctuated here and again by the dark green of cypress trees; the other was an urban view over what are perhaps some of the world's loveliest buildings, the Cathedral and Battistero, and the ochre and coral city of Florence itself.

The garden of the villa had been neglected, but with her usual blend of charm and efficiency, Mrs Keppel soon had her gardeners competing to indulge her every whim. Before long, begonias blossomed and huge tubs of gardenias and syringa lined the terraces, so fragrant that an elderly English colonel complained that they were quite improper! Mrs Keppel transformed the house inside as well, bringing from Grosvenor Street her famous Chinese pagodas and screens.

During the 'Twenties and 'Thirties, the Keppels entertained constantly at L'Ombrellino. There are endless photographs in Edwardian houseparty style, of glamorous and long-forgotten socialites, deposed royals about whom now few know, and fewer care, visiting Infantas and flower-like débutantes with housemaid names, 'Cora', 'Peggy'. Violet appears often, beautifully dressed, relaxed, looking happy and vivacious. Cyril Connolly recalled in the introduction to *Challenge* his first meeting with Violet in Florence at this time.

'She never had a very good figure, her attractiveness centred on her voice which was low and quite bewitching, equally at home in French and English and seldom rising above a husky murmur; her mouth was wide and sensual, her nose rather large, her eyes magnificent and working in close support of her smile to produce an ironical, rather mocking expression. She was an excellent friend.

'I first met her in Florence in 1927. I had been taken to stay with Berenson by his brother-in-law Logan Pearsall Smith, she was at her mother's villa, the Ombrellino. We both discovered we didn't like Florence and cared only for France, which made us conspirators. Violet was older than I, one of the first sophisticated married women I was to meet.

'Violet usually sat with a long cigarette-holder in one hand, a short skirt revealed her elegant crossed legs as in the Blanche portrait, while puns and epigrams bubbled forth in what was really a continuous bilingual word-play. I knew nothing of her role as a queen in Gomorrah, she was more like a literary elder sister. Her husband, Denys Trefusis, I liked immediately, he was charming, graceful and rather dashing, like so many of the men who had returned from the war.'

A full life socially in France and Italy did not prevent Violet from indulging her taste for travelling. She had always had a romantic urge to visit Russia, an urge that had been strengthened by Denys who had been there three times and was fascinating on the subject of all things Russian, and this urge was eventually realised in the summer of 1936 when Violet took a Scandinavian cruise which ended with two weeks in Russia. Sadly for someone whose greatest heroine was Catherine the Great, Russia of 1936 was a complete disappointment. Nothing could have been further from Violet's preconceived ideas. Far from being romantic, Russia was smug. The people seemed indifferent to their lot, accepting without question the awful food, the lack of anything to buy in the shops, the autocratic presence that ruled their lives. Worst of all, one of the supposed highlights of the trip, a visit to Tsarskoe Selo, proved to

Violet just how petty and small-minded the last Tsar (and Tsarina) of all the Russias had been.

'In their tiny island of detached domesticity, the Imperial family led an exemplary, if narrow life. A complacency worthy of the three little pigs defying the Big Bad Wolf, possessed them. They were not interested in Russia. The letters they exchanged might have been posted in Kensington and delivered in Hampstead.

'Viewed through the Empress's Edwardian lorgnette, Rasputin becomes a kind of heroic and misunderstood suffragette; the Metropolitan, a meddlesome vicar. The great winds of the Steppes never so much as ruffled "Sunny's" sleek waves . . .'.[10]

Back in France, Violet wrote two or three articles on her visit to Russia. They were published in *Le Temps*. An unexpected outcome of this was that she was commissioned to do an interview with Mussolini. This took place the following spring. Violet's most polished version of their meeting is in *Don't Look Round*. Warned that she could expect half an hour with the dictator, if she were extremely lucky, she was with him an hour and twenty minutes. The meeting began inauspiciously enough when Violet skidded on the highly-polished floor and dropped her handbag which immediately burst open and scattered the intimacies of her life all over the room. 'We met on all fours, face to face, under the writing table.' Perhaps this broke the ice, but the interview was certainly a success ending only when Il Duce's meagre dinner was brought in on a tray. Mussolini presented Violet with a chewed stump of pencil as a memento of her visit. This treasure, in its wooden box, was stolen from St Loup during the Second World War.

Violet's love of fantasy took a specific form in the summer of 1937 when she held a fancy dress ball at the Eiffel Tower. Warned that her guests would probably be pelted with rotten eggs on arrival, Violet was not to be diverted. The ball was staged in honour of the Tower's inauguration in 1889, and her guests were to come dressed in the fashions of the period. Despite the gloomy forecasts, the ball was a resounding success, no Communist demonstrations marring the evening. Paris, that June night, was *en fête* in honour of Violet's birthday, literally and figuratively at her feet.

The memory of the Eiffel Tower Ball grew more precious over

the next two years as the situation in Europe began to draw inexorably to its logical conclusion, the high spot in a glittering decade that had brought Violet so many of the things she craved in life. The approaching war brought her to stock-taking.

'I was at the apex of my life. Literary fumblings were at an end. I had poise, experience, friends, possessions. Romance was, at long last, disciplined, *coups de tête*, rationed. Then, as ever, I believed in three things: God, France, my mother.'[11]

Violet was at St Loup when war was declared. Then for months nothing happened. All of a sudden, back in Paris and working for the Red Cross, she found she had half an hour to get ready to leave. She had no chance of going back to St Loup (on the direct line of invasion) but set out for the Dordogne with her friend, the Princesse de Chimay. Terrified for her parents in Italy, Violet was greatly relieved to find telegrams waiting for her on arrival at Gilone de Chimay's house near Bergerac. The Keppels had arrived in Cannes. Violet wired them to meet her forthwith at Bordeaux. But the Keppels did not seem to realise the seriousness of the situation and after wasting another week at Cannes, wired Violet to meet them at Dax, near Bayonne. Thinking that it would be possible to get a boat there, Violet set off. On arrival, she heard of the invasion of Paris and the fall of France, disastrous news to one who loved France so dearly. She could hardly believe her ears, and when she did, could not accept the indignity suffered by her beloved adopted country.

Meanwhile things were becoming desperate for the three of them. At Bayonne, Violet discovered that the last boat for England had left and that their only hope was to cross the border into Spain, travel to Portugal, and hope to get a boat there.

Visas for Spain were more or less impossible to obtain unless one could pull strings. Violet had a good string – she knew the Spanish ambassador in Paris, and he was at Bordeaux. She set off post-haste. The news at Bordeaux was not encouraging. Apparently M. de Lequerica spent the whole time when he was not on the telephone to Hitler, on the telephone to Mussolini. Violet tried not to be disheartened. After a night in an abandoned house, she went to the Spanish consulate. The house was besieged by hundreds of people, all bent on the same errand. Her case seemed hopeless. Then she happened to catch sight of the ambassador's private secretary, a man whom she had met several times in Paris. By the greatest good luck, he saw her and mimed that she should write a note. The note was written, and handed to a soldier. After an interminable wait, her name was called. Once inside, another interminable wait seemed unimportant. Eventually M. de Lequerica appeared and Violet was given her precious visas.

Rushing back to Biarritz, where the Keppels had taken refuge, (one wonders what Edwardian nostalgia the place aroused in Alice Keppel), Violet pondered her next move: how to get visas for Portugal. Unfortunately she had no strings at all to pull. But Gilone de Chimay, who had arrived to join her, was a distant connection of the Portuguese consul at Bayonne. The two lay in wait at his opulent villa and, in a positively Firbankian scene, Violet describes their reception by a distant cousin of Madame de Chimay – Bebecita, clad in purple silk pyjamas, dispensing champagne, and discussing hordes of distant relatives.

After all this, on arrival at Biarritz, waving the precious visas in a glow of achievement, Violet was met by her father. '"We won't need those now. There is a boat leaving for England tonight. Just time to pack your things!"'

In a black misery of heart, Violet prepared to leave France. In the chaos of embarkation, she managed to lose her entire collection of jewellery, handing the bag it was in in error to a porter who then disappeared into the night. Three miserable days were spent on board, before they sailed, and once they did, there was the terror of German submarines, and German warships lying in wait for them. Violet felt she had hit rock bottom. 'I had lost my home, my friends, my possessions, and last, but not least, my identity. I was the Woman without a Past. Nothing remained but to turn over a new leaf.'[12]

[8]

The unexploded bomb

To some extent Violet was right when she called herself a Woman without a Past. People had more important things to think about in 1940 than the scandal which had driven Violet away from her native country nearly twenty years before. Her arrival in England, therefore, much to her relief, was anticlimactic. The presence of her parents smoothed over any awkwardness there might be, and it was not long before Violet was picking up the threads of a long-forgotten life. She had kept in touch with many of her old friends and renewing contact with them helped a little to forget what was happening over the Channel.

But to one particular person the news of Violet's arrival was not received with such equanimity. Vita Sackville-West had very mixed feelings. In a letter dated 12th September 1940, from Sissinghurst Castle in Kent, she wrote:

'Curious how war has drawn the strands of our lives together again. I was so worried about you when France collapsed; I couldn't bear to think of you in danger and distress. One travels far, only to come round to the old starting-point. I realised that we might still be sitting on the leather fire-seat at 30 Portman Square, when I went home to Hill Street saying to myself, like an incantation "I have a friend. I have a friend".

'And thousands of other things as well.'

She could sympathise up to a point with Violet's feeling of homelessness, but she knew Violet only too well:

'You sound so unhappy, my sweet; I do mind. It doesn't surprise me to hear that your life is full of complications. I've never known it to be anything else, but you used to like to choose them for yourself and now they must have rather taken charge.'[1]

In the intervening years, Vita had withdrawn into her own world, a world shared by Harold Nicolson at weekends, a world which encompassed Virginia Woolf, but a quiet withdrawn world where writing and making gardens were the major preoccupations. Like Lady Slane, Vita's heroine of *All Passion Spent* published some ten years earlier, Vita 'had had enough of bustle, and of competition, and of one set of ambitions writhing to circumvent another. She wanted to merge with the things that drifted into an empty house, although unlike the spider she would weave no webs. She would be content to stir with the breeze and grow green in the light of the sun, and to drift down the passage of years, until death pushed her gently out and shut the door behind her. She wanted nothing but passivity while these outward things worked their will upon her.'

Vita's mood of similar passivity was part of her way of life and the reappearance of Violet could only be a threat to such a life especially since Violet seemed intent on playing some of the old cards, causing Vita to react in a way she found alarming.

'I got a letter from you today. Yes, of course (idiot that you are) it upsets me to see you or hear your voice. I hate you for having this effect on me. I resent knowing that if I were suddenly to see a photograph of you it would disturb me for at least 24 hours.

'Damn you. You have bitten too deeply into my soul. I love you perennially in the odd way we both realize. That doesn't mean that I trust you – or would ever commit myself to you again. I know better than that now. But I do love you.'[2]

Later on in the letter she discusses a suggestion of Violet that their story might be written.

'How much I would like to talk to you about this – quite dispassionately and with all the objective intelligence that you and I could bring to bear on it. I only wish that I could trust myself (and you) to come and stay with you.

'But I don't, so I won't.'

This theme was an echo of Vita's letter of 27th January 1941.

'As I said, I write in a bad temper. My world, my life, is getting complicated at this moment and I hate that. I really hate that.

'And that is one of the reasons I don't want to get involved with you again: I really dislike the complications and intrigues that your life entails. They bore me.

'I loved you, and shall always love you, but I could never be bothered with all your maze and labyrinth of life.

'I don't want to fall in love with you all over again.'[3]

Violet saw Sissinghurst for the first time in the summer of 1941. It reminded her of her beloved St Loup, and through her homesickness she was able to be amused by the fact that they had both acquired towers as their homes. "*Chacun sa tour.*"

After the visit, Vita confessed in a letter to Violet how alarming she found it that Violet's spell was still as potent as ever:

'We simply couldn't have this nice, simple, naif, childish connexion without its turning into a passionate love-affair again.

'If you have any honesty in your nature, you will agree with me.

'You and I can't be together. I go down country lanes and meet a notice saying "Beware. Unexploded bomb!"

'So I have to go round another way.

'You are the unexploded bomb to me.

'I don't want you to explode.

'I don't want you to disrupt my life.

'My quiet life is dear to me. I hate being dragged away from it.

'This letter will anger you. I don't care if it does, since I know that no anger or irritation will destroy the love that exists between us.

'And if you really want me, I will come to you, always, anywhere.

'You see, you said we might have two sorts of capital to draw on: the great tragedy sort and the childhood-friendship sort. That is true in a way – but not wholly true. You know quite well, if you face it honestly, that although the childhood-friendship link between us is strong and important, the other sort matters equally.

Mitya.'[4]

The two middle-aged ladies (Vita was 49, Violet 47) seemed to have put their love into a proper perspective at last. Nothing so dull as mere friendship had survived the cataclysm: they still loved each other deeply with occasional reminders of the flares of passion to throw it into relief. But they were two very different women from the girls they had been twenty years before. It was Violet now who cared what the world had to say; as for Vita, she wanted no disruption in her peaceful existence. Violet was still searching as always for the perfect relationship, and it was comforting to know that Vita still found her nearness unsettling and to think that if she really exerted herself she could rekindle the flame a little. No–one had loved Violet as Vita had, and Violet had never loved as she loved Vita.

Vita apart, there were other compensations in life in exile. To begin with, Violet and her parents went to Sonia in Hampshire, but Mrs Keppel was not a country person at heart and felt much happier at the Ritz, even though bombs might fall all around her. Violet and Sonia's relationship had always been uncertain, and Violet found herself in a dilemma. Not wishing to stay in Hampshire, she was terrified of the bombing in London. Then she hit on a lucky solution: she would invite herself to stay with Dorothy Walker Heneage in Somerset.

In July 1920, Violet had written to Vita:

'I do think Dorothy an attractive woman. She is so whimsical, illusive, capricious,' "volontaire", vehement, passionate in her likes and dislikes. (She is not unlike me.) And what I adore is her complete and thorough frankness.'

In *Don't Look Round* Violet gives a delightful description of the châtelaine of Coker Court, a beautiful part Tudor, part Georgian house overlooking Somerset and Dorset. Though she had not seen her for many years, the understanding that had existed between them was quite strong enough to withstand the unexpected proposal of an extended visit. The friendship continued from the point where it had been abandoned.

Houses and surroundings had ever been of major importance in ensuring Violet's peace of mind, and at Coker Court everything contributed towards restoring Violet to a more equable mood. Completely enervated by the strain of the preceding months, the traumatic upheaval of leaving France, a long stay in the country to gather herself together was exactly what was needed. Violet's description of her Somerset sojourn has a distinctly Cranford ring about it: shopping trips to Yeovil, tea with the vicar (who incidentally had fallen madly in love with her), and the daily doings of the locals.

According to Derek Hill, such was the impression Violet made on the vicar as she appeared in church one week beautifully dressed, in a stunning hat, that he announced it was the third Sunday after Ascot, instead of Advent! Violet had met Derek in London when she was staying at the Ritz with her mother, but came to know him well while he was farming in Wiltshire as he frequently cycled over to Coker for Saturday and Sunday. In 1945, he did a 'joke portrait' of her in one of her Paris hats. Violet threatened to sue him if he ever exhibited it.

After a long stay at Coker Court, Violet decided to set up her own home, and took the Manor House at West Coker. The house outside was beautiful: inside it was filled with hideous bric-à-brac. Kind friends soon banished the worst of this to the cellars, and in its place lent pictures and antiques. All knew how important it was for Violet to have beautiful objects around her.

With the house came a cook-housekeeper and a daily woman. Mrs Clark, the cook-housekeeper, was strictly a meat-and-two-veg. kind of cook but what she lacked in knowledge she soon made up for in enthusiasm. Within weeks, she was embarking on the most ambitious of continental dishes. Not even rationing could dampen her zeal.

For nearly five years Violet enjoyed her country life: becoming involved in the local scene, making new friends, watching the birds, observing the creeping advances of English springs, bringing *cordon bleu* to West Coker.

She started to write another book, something different from the novels she had written before. This was *Prelude to Misadventure*, a book of memoirs, dedicated to 'those faithful French who have left their homes and their families in order to fight on our side'. Many of the pieces contained in the book were to appear again in *Don't Look Round* ten years later, either condensed, or varied by endings that the war had brought about. Violet's faith in the stubborn, unyielding nature of her beloved France pours from the pages; in temporary subjection to German occupation, her adopted country would never give up. In one piece, 'Made in Germany', she compares France to the aloof and disdainful Marianne, while

Germany, a vulgar parvenu, longs for an elegant mistress to advertise his wealth.

'Thanks to her he thinks he will be admitted into the best society. No longer will the Elite of Europe turn up its nose at him, Marianne must submit to his loathsome caresses, or – be silenced for ever. Marianne will *pretend* to submit, but secretly, like Judith, she will sharpen her sword, waiting until the Teutonic Holophernes, sated and somnolent, lays his befuddled head on her knees, then –'

Descriptions of some special French friends (Paul Reynaud, the de Chambruns, Anna de Noailles, and Princesse Marthe Bibesco) and acquaintances make up part of the book, and there is an account of the famous interview with Mussolini which was to appear in a more polished version in *Don't Look Round*. Travels before the war are recounted: to Russia, and Budapest. The acquisition of her country house at St Loup (called in this book Guermantes) is described, and her chaotic escape from France with her parents.

Writing about France helped diminish the despondency of not being able to be there. It also helped when various French friends arrived from time to time with first-hand news – Colonel Gaston Palewski, General de Gaulle's right-hand man, and General Catroux, who caused a sensation at the station in his uniform and medals. French and English would meet at Violet's house at weekends. 'West Coker . . . is one of the few places where I have the sensation of being back in Europe, not on an isolated self-opinionated island,' wrote Joan Haslip from London.

Violet joined the Fighting French presided over by an old friend, Lady Crewe. With Leslie Hore-Belisha, a new friend, she agonized over the fate of France. Looking at her adopted country from a distance, she could clearly see the way in which it had shaped her destiny. Never, she concluded, could she have been a writer had she stayed in England. It takes the French to keep one up to the mark, with their implacable questions: '*Qu'est-ce que vous préparez?*' '*C'est pour quand?*'

News arrived from time to time from friends Violet had left behind in France. The Duchesse d'Harcourt was arrested by the Gestapo for belonging to the Resistance, and put into prison where she was so badly treated that she died shortly after her release. At the beginning of 1945 she wrote Violet a letter which must have brought a lump to the throat.

'Few things to tell you from here. The Gautiers are at St Loup, which you will find has suffered only very little. As for me, I live between Paris Maisons and Le Calliage des Roches where the boys are now – all this going on with almost intolerable transport difficulties. Still, we must be patient! I would so much like to see you again, my god, I have so many things to tell you. There is a song which we sang in prison which began like this: "When you see your village again" and I often think that St Loup will also be my village.

'I kiss you lovingly. . . .

Antoinette.'[5]

Cyril Connolly was a friend Violet had made years before in Florence. When he started to edit the magazine *Horizon*, it was natural that he should ask her to be a contributor. In June 1943, *Horizon* published a short story by Violet entitled *The Carillon*.

Set in the winter of 1940, the story is Violet's expression of the indomitable nature of France. The plot is simple: a terrifying old duchess dies, and the family attends the funeral. The rituals attending the ceremony, the back-biting after the frugal funeral feast has been consumed, the eternal and inevitable family squabbles: these continue reassuringly just the same despite the horrors, the dead husbands and sons, the pacing German sentries outside the door, lack of food, of heat, the disruption of the settled order and comfort of the old life. The chimes of the castle clock measure the hours, the days, unchanging and unalterable, 'like the soul of France, icily aloof, impregnable, enduring'.

Violet had an unusual gift of seeing in her mind's eye every written word as a symbol in relation to any other word that looked at all like it. Her writing is full of alliteration, rhymes and eye-rhymes, of almost identical words, plus or minus a letter. 'Her domed, doomed family forehead', 'there are degrees of blackness, of crêpiness, of creepiness' are two examples in *The Carillon*. But there is one composition which even more particularly illustrates this virtuosity, the piece which *Horizon* published in November of the same year, *Triptych*. The essay compares and contrasts the three countries that Violet knew so well: England, France and Italy.

It is quite brilliant in miniature, the words are like hailstones tumbling down in a scintillating cascade, the juxtaposition of each single syllable deliberate, the effect quite breathtaking.

One of the happier aspects of Violet's enforced stay in England was being able to see a great deal of her parents. For some months they stayed at Coker Court; within days, needless to say, the entire local population was subjugated by Mrs Keppel's charm. In fact, she is still remembered in that quiet corner of Somerset.

Life in the country was enlivened from time to time by visits to London. On one occasion, travelling back to Yeovil by train, Violet was alone in the compartment with a plump businessman who, when asked what he did, replied that he was 'a great lover'. Unfortunately, this exciting piece of information proved to be false, much to Violet's disappointment. He had in fact said he was 'a great glover', Yeovil being the centre of the glove-making industry.

In London, two hostesses of the old world still reigned, although in very different circumstances from formerly. The first of these was Lady Cunard (christened Maud, she changed her name to Emerald as, presumably, being more glamorous, a change which provoked Mrs Keppel to remark, 'Oh but why Emerald dear? There is nothing *green* about you!'). Throughout the war, she continued to entertain at the Dorchester Hotel, where she lived. For a few hours, her guests might forget there was a war raging. There were many who had cause to be grateful to her for her gallant attempt to keep up the old standards of hospitality. Lobster and champagne might be in short supply, but brilliant conversation and rational thought were not.

Tiny and sparkling, Lady Cunard presided over her dinner table with a featherlight touch.

'Emerald gets gay on one sip of cherry brandy and pours forth stories helter-skelter, wholly unpremeditated, in an abandoned, halting enquiring manner that appears to be ingenuous, and is deliberate. Her charm can be devastating.'[6]

On one occasion, when Violet was dining with Lady Cunard, she arrived in London in the middle of an air-raid and in the panic of the moment, left most of her luggage at the station. The entire personnel of the Ritz seemed to have been involved in its recovery, and Violet overheard the prize remark of the night-porter to a colleague: 'Well, we've 'ad V.1., we've 'ad V.2., we've *'eard* of V.D. but in my opinion, V.T. is the worst of the lot!'

Lord Berners contrasted the parties of Lady Colefax, the other well-known hostess of the time, with those of Lady Cunard. 'The first was a party of lunatics presided over by an efficient trained hospital nurse; the second a party of lunatics presided over by a lunatic.'[7]

Violet was not warm in her praises of Lady Colefax. This lady had an unfortunate habit of inviting her guests by a series of dictatorial postcards which was presumably why she always referred to her guests of honour by initials only. She was hoist by her own petard when she went hot-foot to meet the 'P.O.W.' at a lunch party, only to encounter, instead of the Royal Personage himself, the Provost of Worcester!

Violet had of course known Harold Nicolson for twenty-five years or so, but during the war she perhaps came to see what had held Vita's love for her husband for so long. Harold was living in London *en garçon*, returning to Sissinghurst for Saturday to Monday each week from where he went back to the Temple laden with baskets of flowers from the garden. During the week, he and Violet often met at dinner parties. There were two favourite topics of conversation: France and grand cooking. But Harold could never forgive Violet for what had happened so many years before. She had so nearly wrecked his marriage and taken away his beloved Vita.

Violet had first met Robin McDouall when she was staying at the Dorchester Hotel a few years earlier when he was just down from university and working behind the reception desk. Some fifteen years younger than Violet, Robin had joined the volunteer reserve of the Royal Air Force in 1938 and was at this time running a branch of the Air Ministry in London. During the war, Violet and Robin became great friends, seeing each other almost daily when she was in London, sharing the same jokes and both greatly appreciative of good food. From time to time, Violet would be instructed by her mother to invite Robin to one of the dinner parties which she was having at the Ritz. On one occasion, when Violet telephoned, Robin had to apologise that on that occasion he would not be in uniform.

'Oh, but Robin,' wailed Violet, 'you know I love uniforms — uniforms, auburn hair, waterfalls, and double-barrelled names — just like a governess!'

The loving friendship that grew between them lasted the rest of her life. To Robin McDouall, Violet was very good-looking, although her make-up could be a 'little impressionistic'. She was always beautifully dressed, and a wonderful dancer, light on her feet, despite being rather large.

Another exile from France was Violet's old friend, Princesse de Polignac. They met from time to time and the princess came to visit Violet at her Manor House in Somerset. The princess died in London on 26th November 1943 at her flat in Park Lane.

Lady Cunard's favourite confidant was Don Antonio Gandarillas. He was one of Violet's too. Hours were spent gossiping on the telephone. Violet says in *Don't Look Round*, 'No woman in her senses would ever be without him. Neither was I.' Tony Gandarillas was Chilean by birth but lived most of his life in France. He had kept a flat in Paris before the war when Violet originally met him, and during the war he lived in a beautiful house in Cheyne Walk, where Violet was a frequent visitor. His mother had been one of the first to buy paintings by Picasso, hence his friendship with the painter, and he was also a close friend of John Singer Sargent and Cecil Beaton. At Cheyne Walk, Violet heard all the news about her old friends from France as well as meeting some new faces. Tony Gandarillas was addicted to opium, and this gave his conversation more than a touch of fantasy, much appreciated by Violet who really preferred the truth heavily embroidered.

Of all the new friends that Violet made during the war, Betty Richards was the most important. In fact, they had met in Paris before the war, but had never been close friends. Betty was married to reputedly the best-looking man in England, Nigel Richards, who was the real-life inspiration for the anti-hero of Cyril Connolly's book *The Rock Pool*. He was killed in 1942 and Betty lived alone in Dorset with her small daughter, Emma.

Betty was 34, tall, blonde and slender. In Paris, she had been a mannequin at Chanel, and she too spoke fluent French. Violet and Betty shared many interests in common, apart from love of France, including an appreciation of beautiful china of which Betty had an interesting collection. Betty's small house was rather overtaken by her china collection, and Violet draws a fine word picture of the 'belle in the china shop' as she described the angular and amusing collector. Betty liked to tease Violet about her appetite, but since her farming interests meant she had access to cream and eggs, she was able to indulge Violet a little in this.

Like many of Violet's loves, this one was to suffer occasional breakdowns of communication from time to time, but Betty remained one of the most important people in Violet's life. Her enormous sense of fun gave her the ability to laugh at Violet with Violet, in a way at which Violet could not take offence. In *Don't Look Round*, Violet is reticent about her feelings for Betty, partly because before the book was published, Betty married another West Country friend, Colonel Bill Batten. Colonel Batten had at one time been rather a beau of Violet; she describes his qualities in *Don't Look Round* as 'modesty, loyalty, courage, discretion'.

This was high praise. Englishmen usually scored no points with Violet: dim and sentimental were adjectives she usually employed. 'Simplicity, in my eyes, is apt to be as suspect as the Englishman who swears he has nothing to declare. England would never have acquired the nickname of "perfidious Albion" had not a deplorable, a dastardly innocence occasionally peered out of tired blue eyes of septuagenarian British statesmen suddenly overcome with nostalgia for their collection of stamps, or butterflies, or merely the thud of their retriever's tail in the night watches.'[8]

When, later, Betty decided to marry her colonel, she wrote to Violet who was by that time in Italy:

'I shall never, *can* never, could never stop loving you my dear heart but try, will you, to wish me a little luck in an undertaking that so many people approve of, so it seems, so very outstandingly and whole-heartedly. No: I am not "IN LOVE" – but it is difficult at least for me being the sort of person I am, with my standards, and ultimate principles, NOT to love, *very dearly*, so sweet and true a person. What you said about my qualities, darling, was infinitely flattering *but*, if, as you allege, I have WIT – I shall not lose it: ("WIT RUSTETH NOT, IS NOT DECAYED", a paraphrase you will recognize of course?) but the qualities of the person I am about to marry *are*, it seems to me? above the price of rubies? Please, dear heart, be good and wise and gentle: try, too, to "put [in] as much as you want to get out" – as your Mama said, won't you?'

After the war, Betty became a frequent visitor to St Loup and L'Ombrellino, often travelling with Emma, and sometimes accompanied by Robin McDouall. He recalls an occasion at St Loup when they were all at lunch, their last meal before departing for the south. Violet was trying hard to make them stay another day or so, telling all her most amusing stories, and doing her imitations. Betty and Robin were familiar with these little pieces: the bored Harrods' shop assistant, the rich American woman 'doing' Paris, and so on, but Emma was fascinated. Finally, Violet turned her back and when she faced them again, she had put her pearl earrings on her nose, and Emma dissolved into giggles. Betty and Robin laughed too but their laughter was tinged with sadness and guilt that she was trying so hard to make them stay and they could not. It was terribly difficult to ignore the pathetic appeal made by that childlike display.

It was fitting that Violet should first hear of the D–day landings on 6th June, her birthday. She was 50. Nostalgia, so long and so sternly repressed, washed over her.

'An assortment of disconnected objects suddenly appeared before my eyes, in surrealist juxtaposition, the blue letter boxes of Paris, the undulating Art Nouveau lettering of the Métro stations, the thick blue cups of the P.L.M., the black alpaca sleeves of the *employées des Postes*, the blue blouses of the porters, the little girls with gold rings in their prematurely pierced ears, the concierge's crocheted shawl, her fat sated cat: "Cordon s.v.p.". I heard the clang of the *porte-cochère*, the imprecations and hootings of the taxi chauffeurs, the shuffling of small black larvae carrying other people's dresses in the *maisons de couture*. It was too good to be true. I was back in France.'[9]

It was to be a year before she could return in the flesh, however, but it was a year she put to good use, broadcasting to France from the BBC on various subjects. One talk described the contribution made to the arts by the Sitwells and, in another, entitled '*Les francophiles*', Violet paid tribute to Harold Nicolson.

I could not stress too much the services rendered to France by Harold Nicolson, the most eloquent of its interpreters who, by his temperament, his culture and his spontaneous spirit, is better able than anyone to understand the French.[10]

She also referred to Duff Cooper and Raymond Mortimer.

Violet spent most of her time in London now: Somerset was losing its rural charm. The unhurried pace of life in the West Country which had had such a beneficial effect on a bruised spirit was out of joint. The house was given up, traps put together, fond farewells said. Violet was impatient to be gone.

It was during this period in her life that Violet became the sort of person about whom people loved to talk and tell jokes. Even now her friends each have their own particular Violet story, which they will recount with relish. Years before, Denys was supposed to have said to her, 'Cease strutting in front of the looking-glass. . . . We are not taken in. You are like someone who owns a really good picture of which she will only exhibit a shoddy reproduction; why aren't we shown the original?' To which Violet replied: 'Because I'm the caretaker.'[11] The highly polished shell now completely hid the vulnerable creature underneath. Outwardly, Violet was a social character: witty, amusing, brilliant conversationally in both English and French, a writer of clever, brittle books, conventional, completely at home in the circle in which she moved, a deliberately enigmatic person living a life of flamboyant muddle. Underneath, the 'vagrant nymph' still roamed, 'straying from land to land, from age to age, decking her spirit with any flower she met growing by the way, chastely concerned with the quest of beauty.'[12] Truth and beauty and genius were the ideals of the inner person, but so well hidden were they that most people saw her only as a society character.

Anyone who has been as damaged as Violet had been when her love affair with Vita Sackville-West crashed about her in ruins is unwilling to risk that part of their nature again. Their protection lies in putting up a false front and, in Violet's case, this was so effective that few ever penetrated the exterior and found the real person underneath.

Violet hid behind her reputation. An embryo eccentric, she encouraged and contributed to any stories circulating. Always prone to exaggeration, some of her stories now became positive myths, outrageously amusing. She began to cultivate an aura of mystery. Whose daughter was she really? Hints were given by Violet (not always consistent) and suggestions made by others were not always refuted.

The spoilt little girl in Violet still clamoured for attention. She was a creature who from 'the age of three had exacted homage and protection'. Sadly, she was nearly half a century on from the exquisite child she had been. Her eyes and her wonderful thick hair were lovely still, but fondness of food had not improved her figure.

Delightful children can get away with immoderate behaviour; middle-aged women cannot. The deep love that flourished between Violet and her mother meant that Violet never really grew up. Mrs Keppel, now in her seventies, continued to treat her as a precious little girl, and Violet continued to think of her mother as a superhuman figure holding the strings of destiny in her hand. Violet had no children of her own, and therefore had never had to behave as a responsible adult. She never mastered simple grown-up skills such as punctuality and reliability. Suiting other people's convenience, fitting in with their plans, were completely beyond her scope. She had never been taught them; now it was too late to learn.

People who were fond of Violet called her vagueness unworldliness, her playing with truth fantasy. Those who were not called them utter thoughtlessness and downright lies. There were many who were not at all fond of Violet because of this and, as the years passed, even people who had been devoted to her became less willing to have anything to do with some of her more extreme vagaries.

The Violet legend grew as time went on and Violet never tried to live it down. On the contrary, she fostered her reputation, encouraged the jokes and the stories by exceeding in real life what occurred in fantasy. Perhaps being a character, a grand eccentric, is a compensation, a consolation prize for all the struggles one has lost. It is certainly better than being overlooked.

Violet would never live up to her name and shrink satisfactorily. Colette was absolutely right: Geranium would have been far more suitable.

[9]
A great lady

When eventually the long-awaited permission arrived, Violet immediately set off by boat train to France. She found her precious country superficially immensely changed but at the same time, reassuringly just the same underneath. The landscape she glimpsed from the train from Dieppe to Paris was scarred by war; there were starving children clamouring for any scraps of food from the travellers; there was all the inconvenience and discomfort of a country trying to return to normal, but she was back. That was all that really mattered. There was one enormous bonus: since the autumn of 1946 the new ambassador to Paris had been Duff Cooper, whose wife, Lady Diana, had been a lifelong friend of Violet. The British Embassy was the centre of the revival in social life, and it provided Violet with a friendly base.

Paris itself seemed hardly to bear the marks of war. A bullet hole here and there bore witness to occupation but to Violet these blemishes served only to enhance the beauty of her favourite city. Ecstatic, in a borrowed car, she spent her first day driving about. That evening at a party given for her by Lady Diana at the British Embassy, she found many of her old friends, undaunted by the past or by the future.

The future that faced them was nearly as grim as the recent past. On a purely physical level, food of most kinds was in extremely short supply and there was no fuel for heating. Houses were freezing. There was no hot water and baths were a luxury that existed only in imagination.

But there were compensations. The great avenues were practically empty of traffic, the sun streamed down through the large windows, in the great squares the chestnuts were coming out, and there were all the threads of an old life to pick up. Violet had lunch with Jean Cocteau and dinner with her old friends, the de Chambruns. She began to gather what life during the occupation had been like.

Desperately anxious to visit St Loup, and yet horribly nervous at what she might find when she arrived, Violet had to rely on the same kind friend who had met her at the Gare du Nord, since the train service was still practically non-existent. On the third day after her arrival, the visit was made, Violet sitting withdrawn and brooding beside her driver. '*A la recherche du temps perdu*, what would I find at the other end? Nothing is more unpleasant than the knowledge that one's home has been occupied by the enemy; what I did not know was that their favourite occupation consisted in dressing-up in my underclothes in which they strutted up and down the dining-room table. A monocled Colonel applauded this ravishing bevy of young homosexuals.'[1]

They arrived. At least the house was still standing and the couple who had looked after it, and Violet, for so many years came out to greet her. Strange doings at German-occupied St Loup appeared to have unhinged their minds, but in a harmless way. The worst was the damage to the contents and that was not serious except for a few precious books that had been stolen and some German slogans scrawled over the walls. At least the furniture was intact.

In the village, life was slowly returning to normal. One casualty of the war had been the village church bell, and in, to English minds, typical French fashion, a committee was formed to arrange for a replacement. The installation of the new bell was a lengthy business, complicated by the rivalry of two local dressmakers who both claimed the sole right to make the bell's christening robe. Violet achieved a compromise, and the bell was eventually hoisted into position.

Violet compared St Loup with the Somerset village she had left.

'Here there are no flowers, save the ogreish zinnias, no pets (I suspect these of having been eaten), no jokes; there is no competition, no archness, no complacency. Each household is solely occupied with the struggle for life, the pitiful scramble for uncertain rations, which few in England except the half-famished, would condescend to eat. The daily menu consists of ersatz coffee (grilled acorns mixed with barley), watery soup in which float a few onions and carrots, potatoes are a scarcity; occasionally a little chalky cheese, and even more exceptionally, a nugget of rancid butter; true, there is the weekly meat ration, but it is grossly inadequate. The interior of these cottages is significant: you instinctively look for the cosy clutter of their British counterparts, the potted fern, the caged bullfinch or canary, the tabby on the hearth, the innumerable souvenirs, wireless set, glossy mahogany sideboard.

'Here, apart from utilitarian pots and pans, a few flyblown photographs, there is nothing. . . .

'The first person to greet me on my return was the Communist Mayor (an old friend) with a plate of freshly-picked plums and some professional advice about my neglected vine. We are at present contemplating the joint purchase of a tandem with which to do our shopping in Provins.'[2]

The £75 allowance which Violet had been able to bring into France ran out, and she had to return to London until her French money account had been settled. This took some time.

Christmas 1945 was spent at the Ritz with her parents. Violet was suffering from jaundice and spent most of her time discussing with her mother how they would spend 1946. The Villa dell'Ombrellino had also miraculously survived the war, and Mrs Keppel was suffering in the same way as Violet had from both yearning and dreading to return. She had at least received some first-hand news of its fate from a British Army officer who had visited it late in 1944. This was a Major Hamish Erskine, an erstwhile fiancé of Nancy Mitford. His news was of course terrifically exciting, less good was his timing.

'. . . A sunburnt, travel-stained young man burst into my mother's bedroom at the Ritz, in the early hours of the morning.

'He was Major Hamish Erskine, M.C., just arrived from Florence.

'"Mrs Keppel, Mrs Keppel," he exulted, "I can't wait to tell you that the Villa is safe, everything is intact, even the Chinese pagodas!"

'This was altogether too much. My mother disliked being taken
by surprise; besides, by then, my parents, by mutual consent, had
"buried" the Villa. It was exactly as though they had decently
mourned a relative for years, only to be told now that the relation
was alive and kicking.

'"Those, my dear Hamish," my mother replied with *hauteur*,
"those were the *common pagodas*!"

'Hamish and I both subsequently agreed that no term of
opprobrium could be more effective; threateningly ambiguous, it
gave one furiously to think: "She was nothing but a common
pagoda! O you common pagoda, you!"

'Of course, as soon as this wonderful piece of news had been
properly assimilated, they were overcome with joy. The curtain we
had thought drawn for ever, parted: Florence, a terrace overlooking
the town, orange and lemon trees in tubs, the air vibrates with a
jangle-tangle of bells . . .'.[3]

It was March 1946 before Violet could return to Paris. In the
meantime, the reassuring return to normal had continued. The
single-page *Figaro* was now managing a four-page edition once a
week. The Louvre had reopened. The Black Market flourished in
Paris, but at least in the country it was possible to buy fresh meat
and vegetables and dairy produce from friendly farmers at
reasonable prices. Some houses actually had heating and hot water
and the end of the month brought a warm spell and bright blue skies
which were more inspiring than anything.

At Reboux, the great milliner's shop, Madame Lucienne was
back in business. As certain as the seasons themselves, every spring
and every autumn, the fashionable beat a path to Reboux. In the
world of haute couture, a new name was about to break. Susan
Mary Alsop wrote to her friend Marietta Tree from Paris in
February of the following year: 'The girl friends say I must have a
look at a man called Christian Dior, no-one ever heard of him before
but there is something called "The New Look" which he has
invented.'[4] In later years Christian Dior became a friend of Violet
and was a visitor at L'Ombrellino.

It was in this year that Violet acquired Alice, lady's maid,
secretary and Mistress of the Robes. This formidable person

became utterly indispensable to Violet, partly because she understood her mistress and was prepared to put up with her vagaries and stand up to her when the occasion demanded, but also because she had all the fundamental, and particularly French qualities, that Violet lacked: thrift, organisational ability, common sense. From now on, Alice was always in the background, a power in the household, feared by the other servants, but a stalwart when it came to arranging Violet's life.

At St Loup, the usual state of things was almost once again established. The slogans had been painted over, the neglected garden lovingly replanted, and even some of the precious antiques had been replaced. Violet's life was resuming its normal chaotic disorder, provoking from Mrs Keppel one of her rare protestations. She was at the Palace Court Hotel in Bournemouth, where life was not so exhilarating.

'I got a letter from you this morning, dated April 12th but it had no ending, except about manure, for St Loup, and there were no loving messages, and it was not *even signed*. Darling, what has happened to your letters? I can only suppose you wrote something on another sheet of paper and did not send it with the letter, but I do like getting your love.'

Violet set off on an expedition to collect her silver which the Duc d'Harcourt had taken away in a Red Cross ambulance at the start of the war and hidden in the cellars of his castle in Toulouse where it had remained unmolested. Grateful Violet later presented the duke with a service of *vermeil* which had belonged to Catherine the Great.

'Far from being corroded by the damp, as I had feared, [the silver] revealed itself, when unpacked, to be in mint condition. We packed it up again in numerous cardboard boxes, preparatory to taking it back to Paris. The packing was neither aesthetic nor secure. When I boarded the train, the conductor informed me, with a twinkle in his eye, that I was sharing my compartment with a monsieur who was getting in at Cahors. Would it not be possible, I expostulated, for the monsieur to be put with another monsieur? No, all the sleepers were taken, it was out of the question. Besides, he added with a leer, "*Sait-on jamais, ce monsieur sera peut-être charmant?*" I cast an apprehensive look at my bulging boxes. Perhaps le monsieur, not content with being *charmant*, would also be an amateur of old silver?

'However, there was nothing to be done about it. The conductor was clearly a passionate reader of *romans feuilletons*, and hoped for the worst. There was no concealing the cardboard boxes, or their contents. A Queen Anne teaspoon was already peeping out of one of them. In despair, I concealed them as best I could.

'Then I had a brain-wave. I whisked out my lip-stick, and rubbed it all over my face and hands, lay down, and composed myself for sleep. Some two hours later, the train stopped. The door of my compartment opened, the light was switched on, a stifled shriek, a panic-stricken bang. I was left alone with my silver.'[5]

In Paris, people were beginning to give parties again. Food and heating were still in short supply, but people were ready to crowd into crowded rooms to meet their friends and talk. Betty Richards came to stay. 'I had a long letter from Betty. She has been *most* kind, she adored Paris, and longs to live there, the details in her letters must be left to your imagination. You will know what I mean, but it is wiser *not* to *write* such personal matters as the Dr says!!' wrote Mrs Keppel from Sheffield Park, Uckfield. Then solicitously, 'I am so worried about your teeth, darling, isn't your wonderful dentist still in Paris? What is the matter with them? I worry. Let me know soon.'

In August, Alice Keppel visited her daughter en route for Aix-les-Bains where she was to take a cure. It was to be her last visit to Paris, but although Violet was deeply conscious of being in her favourite place with her favourite person, she had no premonition of this. After her visit, Mrs Keppel left for Aix where Violet was to join her a fortnight later. The cure was not a success, too rigorous, it was to treat rheumatism when Mrs Keppel was in fact suffering from sclerosis of the liver. Apart from this, Violet and her mother enjoyed their short holiday together, the last time they were to be alone.

Unable to reserve a sleeper on the same train as her mother, Violet stayed on at Aix-les-Bains, while Mrs Keppel travelled to Florence. When Violet joined her parents at L'Ombrellino, it was

Lady Diana Cooper

to find the house more beautiful than she remembered it, untouched and unaltered by the ravages of war. The only blot was the health of her mother. It was not in Alice Keppel's nature to complain, but it was obvious that she was suffering.

Violet had a special ability not to take in warning signals, a child's way of ignoring what she did not want to see. Her mother had enjoyed glorious good health all her life. It was impossible that it should ever fail her. Indeed, the Florentine sunshine seemed to be repairing the harm of the cure at Aix, and Violet decided to return to France.

As a guest at the British Embassy, Violet was at the very centre. There could be no more glamorous hostess than Lady Diana Cooper.

'Every day a dazzled Paris paid tribute to the beauty and verve of my hostess. She slept in the crimson and gold bedroom of Pauline Borghese, her *petit lever* was in the eighteenth-century manner, a pampered pug on her pillow, an admiring and attentive friend at her bedside, waiting to record the first sally of the day.

'Diana is an inimitable raconteuse: endowed with an excellent visual memory, plus the gift of mimicry, her rendering of a scene, brusque and burlesque, gives one the feeling of a delightful surprise one experiences in looking over the shoulder of a caricaturist. Envy is not one of my shortcomings, yet it was impossible not to envy this woman, who was not only the most beautiful of her generation, but also the funniest.'[6]

Christmas 1946 was spent in London and New Year back in Paris. On New Year's Eve, Jean de Gaigneron held a party at his beautiful flat above Quai Voltaire. Despite the fact that the temperature inside (except in the immediate vicinity of stoves) was almost as low as that outside, the select party, which included the British ambassador and ambassadress, Colonel Palewski and Nancy Mitford, managed to see in the New Year with style, and no little hope that 1947 would achieve some of the political stability that the old year had failed to bring.

'How I wish you, with *all* my heart all happiness, good luck and good health in 1947, and may it bring us *often* together', wrote Mrs Keppel from London on 27th December.

In *Don't Look Round*, Violet described 1946 as her 'last year of unadulterated happiness'. But at the beginning of 1947, she had no premonition of what was in store. A new love affair was taking up her mind and heart, a love affair which had so hopeful an outcome that it was decided a two-week trial marriage would be undertaken as a preliminary to the real thing. Accordingly, a visit was arranged to the vast palace near Cremona of the intended, Guido Sommi Picenardi, Marchese di Calvatore. At first all was wonderful: shared interests and similar traits of character put the lovers in relaxed and happy mood. Then doubt raised its ugly head in Violet's mind. Like Alexa in *Broderie anglaise*, she was frightened of subjugation.

'All went well until the day she became his mistress. From then on she felt herself lost. Civil war erupted between her senses and her brain, cutting off all retreat, replacing her many activities by a lofty preference for doing nothing.'[7]

The vast pile in which he lived was made the scapegoat.

'The place frightened me. It was ostentatiously possessed, like a bride. How could it fail to be jealous of its owner? Clearly it would never consent to be shared with anyone.'[8]

Terrified that her cosmopolitan host would delve too deeply if given too much intimacy, Violet began to suggest sight-seeing trips. Eventually, Guido took offence and the visit ended on the predictably fatal line, 'It would be better if we did not meet for a few months, in order to give our friendship time to recover'. That remark invariably signifies the end.

The love affair had been a distraction from a series of warning signs and red alerts from Florence. Alice Keppel was slowly dying at L'Ombrellino, but with characteristic unselfishness, she did not want to alarm anyone until it was really necessary. Violet had ignored the signs as long as she could through sheer terror, but in the spring of 1947 she hurried to Florence to find matters far advanced, and no hope. The beautiful Tuscan spring ravished a heart already laid bare by the sight of her mother's suffering. There was nothing to be done, except to read to her, try to keep her amused with little domestic stories. There was her father, rushing desperately up and downstairs, despite his heart condition, as helpless as anyone else. In the centre lay Mrs Keppel, serene and considerate to the last.

In the most moving passage in her autobiography, Violet described the death of her beloved mother.

'On the day that was to be her last, in the afternoon, the young gardener next door sang a desultory love song full of frustrated passion. My mother was asked if he should be told to stop. She shook her head. The love song accompanied her almost to the end. All day she had neither eaten nor drunk. "Is there anything you want?" I bent over her despairingly.

'"You," came the whisper, "You."

'Yet, I wasn't with her when she died. It was all over in a minute. When I came in, her head, with its blunt white curls, was buried like a child's in her pillow. "For so He giveth His beloved sleep".'[9]

Alice Frederica Keppel died at Villa dell'Ombrellino on 11th September 1947, and was buried in Florence. A memorial service was held in London at the beginning of October, at which Queen Mary was represented and which Mrs Keppel's friends attended in force. People of all ages had loved Mrs Keppel, as the obituary columns showed. *The Times* spoke of her charm which had 'bewitched the world of rank and fashion of the nineties and early nineteen hundreds', of her 'kindness and consideration' and 'culture and wit'. Sir Osbert Sitwell wrote of 'the special beauty she created' and of how she had been as much loved by the Italians as by her English friends. E.D. described how one 'never heard her say an unkind word and yet how amusing she was; a living example of wit without spite'. But the most affectionate tribute of all was contributed by 'A friend' who summarised what Mrs Keppel had meant to so many people of so many different backgrounds.

'The passing of Mrs George Keppel, perhaps more than the death of any of her contemporaries, puts a full stop to an era. Without being strictly beautiful, judged by exacting canons, she had that indefinable quality compounded of charm, *chic*, dignity, and vitality which caused more strictly beautiful women to be overlooked when she was present. Perhaps no woman of her generation had a readier wit, a keener sense of the ridiculous, and above all a greater genius

for friendship. Although the peak point of her life was at a period
which in many ways witnessed the decline of the aristocratic
principle into vanities, Alice Keppel belonged by temperament and
birth to a generation when great ladies preserved the façade,
entertained magnificently, but without ostentation could converse
realistically in inverted commas instead of employing the language
of the pothouse, and submitted to sometimes irksome rules because
they oiled the wheels of civilised intercourse.

'For many years her long intimacy with the Court and her
acquaintance with men of eminence in every walk of life gave her an
unrivalled knowledge of the *dessous des cartes*. Discretion was
perhaps her long suit, and her great influence was always used to
pour oil on troubled waters. Her tact and realism were combined
with a kindness of heart which became proverbial and not only
made her the least censorious of critics but also found her ever ready
to help those under the shadow of misfortune. The adventurer in
her was ever at the mast-head and her perennial interest in her
fellow-creatures always enabled her to make new friends among the
younger generation. A great friend, a great lady, and a great hostess,
her brilliant, gallant, warm-hearted personality will always be a
joyful memory to the many who knew and loved her.'[10]

Letters and telegrams poured into L'Ombrellino from all
Violet's friends and acquaintances in France, Britain and Italy.
From London, Tony Gandarillas wrote: '*Vous savez chère Violette
combien je vous aime et que le grand malheur que vous frappe me touche
de bien près comme tout ce que vous concerne . . .*'. Betty Richards
wrote at length from the West Country:

'I got in yesterday evening and found your poor wire, and ever
since, I have been wondering *how* I am to write to you, and what I
am to say when I do . . . you mind so much about the spoken word,
and I wish, so much, that I might be blessed with the gift of tongues
and that I might bring you some little comfort, so that I could
convey to you one iota of how full my heart is, and how it is all
yours. It is impossible for *me* to write to *you* the usual trite
conventional phrases, the well-known vernacular of convention, I
know, you see, that love and sorrow are irrational: that the fact that
your mother was no longer young, had had the sort of life that is

Betty Richards

given to few from a superficial aspect, that she had bravely borne
months of weary illness, so that, for her, death must have come as a
relief – all those things, all of them true, cannot make *your* loss any
the less; death is not final for those that have Faith and who believe
in an after life but it can mean a long and heart-breaking separation.
I shall always be proud that your mother treated me as a friend; she
understood me very well in some curious way that bridged the
differences in position, age, conventions, between us; I shall never
forget her turquoise eye when I went to say goodbye for we both
knew that it was for always; I shall never forget her gallantry,
charm, gaiety and warmth, her complete lack of false pride, her
scope, and the particular flavour of her genius and personality. I
shall, too, always remember her trust in me, that she believed in,
trusted and respected me: I shall never forget that I promised her
never to fail you, and nor I will – ever. My greatest regret is that I
am not with you when you most need me, not able to *show* my love
and devotion, not able to succour and support with tenderness. I
would have liked to have paid a last tribute, in person (or by even a
wreath) to a great person, a great lady and a great friend, but even
these sad joys are no longer possible in a world that recognises only
material, only utilitarian, values. Perhaps you may soon be able to
write to me, darling, perhaps not – anyhow I shall understand
either way. Try, *please*, darling, not to "fall out" if only for the fact
that your Maman hated it so; try to remember that no love is ever
wasted; try to believe that my whole heart and faithful devotion are
yours even if my letter is as hopelessly inadequate as I know it to be
– I send you all my love, my heart, my understanding.'

But the most loving tribute of all was Violet's own, her
autobiography, *Don't Look Round*, published in 1952, and dedicated to her mother. It begins with her idyllic childhood and ends
with the death of Mrs Keppel.

'Despair, a persevering pianist, began to decipher the tune that
was likely to drive me insane. At first there were pauses, wrong
notes, then it came, pat, never to cease again.

'Even now, after more than three years, it continues, muted,
piano, piano, just loud enough for me to hear when I am alone. *Je dis
ton nom tout doucement, comme on souffle une chandelle. Nul ne*

m'entend. In losing my mother, I lost everything. She was my youth, I was her old age.'

Her mother's death released Violet from the last restraining hand. She had complete independence. She could go where she wanted, with whom she wanted, buy clothes, houses, antiques, be extravagant in every way, outrage the world. But complete independence was dead sea fruit in her hand. It only accentuated the loneliness.

Apart from the short spell when Violet had been alienated from her mother by her love for Vita Sackville-West, the two had always been on the closest of terms. Mrs Keppel was the only person in the world able to curb the immoderate behaviour of Violet. And she was an artist in the employment of her influence. A trace of sarcasm there, a touch of amusement here, and her daughter immediately saw the error of her ways, even if she did not always change course. 'Oh darling, you *are* lucky! I was never rich enough to buy that', was her only comment on catching sight of an outrageously extravagant James II Monteith. Direct confrontations with Violet were a disaster; making her see the funny side was more likely to succeed. She did not try to change her daughter, knowing that would only defeat its object. She merely used the influence of her own good sense, indicating the sensible alternative, the norm against which all outrageous behaviour would be compared. She did not judge, rage, agonize. That was not her style.

Her style was to influence by example. Her suggestions were practical ones, her criticisms so low-key that it was impossible to take offence.

Alice Keppel had known how to manage her daughter as no-one else ever had or ever would, and when she died, Violet missed her until the day she, too, died.

Her mother had always been the chief support of her life. She was always there to pick up the pieces of her daughter's life whenever calamity struck again. She was responsible for an education that went far beyond the conventional standards of the day. Violet put the fact that she spoke four languages fluently down to her mother, and her extensive knowledge of antiques and objets d'art entirely to her influence and teaching.

Alice Keppel had saved her daughter from complete social ruin by insisting on the marriage to Denys Trefusis, and that Violet stay married to him despite everything. She had tried to make something they could live with out of the loathsome morass of lies and hurt that was their early marriage, and it was her good sense in packing them off to France that saved them from completely destroying one another. It was Mrs Keppel who smoothed over the traces of the scandal of the love affair with Vita Sackville-West, making it possible for her daughter to return to London as a visitor, and during the war. People of all ages had adored her and as a result they were prepared to make allowances for her daughter. The high esteem in which Alice Keppel was generally held shed a soothing all-encompassing light on Violet, who had been permitted her more extravagant behaviour because she was Mrs Keppel's daughter.

Now she was a middle-aged woman, Violet could see what a very different life her mother had charted for her. There she was, the spoilt darling of 16 Grosvenor Street, with the spoils of fortune at her feet: pretty, witty, brilliantly clever, amusing, so articulate, speaking all those languages. Then there was the undoubted cachet of Alice Keppel herself, the distinguished figure of George Keppel, the glories of wealth and position. She was so obviously set to make a brilliant match. Afterwards she would settle down to a life of conventional contentment, bear children, arrange houses, entertain her friends. It was destiny from the cradle.

If Alice Keppel was disappointed in her elder daughter, she never showed it. She never was a snob, and if she had wanted a brilliant marriage, it was because she wanted Violet to be happy, and in practical terms, an assured social position with a man whom one loved was a sure recipe for happiness. She never was a prude, and none knew better than she that love takes many forms. Once she accepted that her daughter preferred women, she merely urged discretion.

But it was because Alice Keppel was the very person she was that Violet remained the unstable person she was. Had she ever had to look after her mother, it might have developed a side of her nature that remained unexploited throughout her life. Her mother had always looked after her, the ever-present influence in the background, the yardstick against which all actions and impulses must be measured. Now that yardstick had gone. And Violet was only too aware of it.

'I can do what I like, go where I wish, there is no one to say me nay. I have what is called "every facility", all the visas. Trespassers will *not* be prosecuted. Fatuous perspectives open up on every side, every house is for sale.

'Assent means absence. (Ascent also means absence.) The unwanted licence of loneliness. Oh, to be hemmed in by frowning family obstacles!'[11]

To Violet, life without her mother stretched ahead meaninglessly. Any achievements did not count without her mother's smiling approval. The sadness is that Violet did achieve something which would have delighted Mrs Keppel: her autobiography.

This is Violet Trefusis at her very best: reminiscing, philosophical, sparkling, malicious, making rapier darts at her friends' reputations, deflating, flattering, flitting from country to country. The book is full of anecdotes: they crowd one another out, each one more outrageous than the last. The famous *tête-à-tête* with Mussolini, can it all really be true? No matter, it makes a wonderful story.

As an alternative to Nancy Mitford's naughty suggestion that the book should be called 'Here Lies Mrs Trefusis', Violet chose the title 'Don't Look Round' which paraphrases one of its most significant passages.

'One is never cured of one's childhood: too happy, as in my case, it exhales an aroma with which the present cannot compete, too unhappy, it poisons life at its source. In either case, it is wiser not to look round.'

Vita Sackville-West is hardly mentioned, apart from a description of their first meeting as children, and *en passant* once or twice. The Princesse de Polignac receives the same treatment. This is no scandalous exposé, it is a book written by a respectable, middle-aged woman, a woman who has lived and enjoyed life to the full, but in whose life now the hot brave passions of youth have no place. It must have been a disappointment for some who hoped for outrageous revelations, but nonetheless, it is a highly readable book, almost as fascinating for what has not been included as for what has.

And, most of all, the character of her cherished mother shines from the pages; it is impossible not to be intermittently dazzled. It is a fitting obituary to such a woman, and a tribute to the talents of her daughter.

Don't Look Round is a wonderfully entertaining readable book. It is an achievement of which her much loved mother would have been justifiably proud.

[10]

To darling Violet

Colonel Keppel only survived his wife by two months. He had always lived in the shadow of his brilliant consort, but he had never given any indication that he resented his supporting role. A gallant soldier, and a man of great charm, he too had his special reputation in Florence. Mrs Jack Leslie, the younger sister of Lady Randolph Churchill, had the wonderful experience of seeing him pointed out to a crowd of open-mouthed sightseers, as 'the lover of Queen Victoria'.[1]

It is doubtful whether the romantic colonel would have appreciated this, as in his later years, his tastes ran to pretty debutantes, to whom he was only too delighted to show the charms of L'Ombrellino. Photographs of his favourites taken in the shadowy beflowered style of his youth adorned his rooms, and his photograph albums depict the beauties of two decades.

He had always been a devoted father, if in Violet's case, sometimes a rather puzzled one. He had been a witness to the extraordinary and distasteful scenes at Amiens when Denys had come to fetch Violet back, and as a true Edwardian, he was shocked to the core by so much public emotional display. In such situations, he appeared curiously helpless. But when it came to arranging the girls' marriages, or marshalling guests at house-parties, he was in his element. Military precision made everything run smoothly and there was never a moment when a guest might be at a loose end.

Violet could quite understand why her father followed her mother so quickly: she felt very much the same.

'He did not wish to survive her. Always the most courteous of men, it was as though he were loth to keep her waiting.

'Puzzled and homeless, he was like a man in a foreign town

without an interpreter. It would have been uncharitable to wish to prolong his life. He went willingly to a secret assignation.'[2]

Completely devastated by the death of her parents, Violet found some consolation in the rearrangement of L'Ombrellino which was now hers for the rest of her life. The contents, the beautiful Chinese screens which Mrs Keppel had brought back from China in 1911 to the house in Grosvenor Street, the Louis XV furniture, even the 'common pagodas', all were dispersed. L'Ombrellino was an enormous house with vast rooms *en enfilade*. It was years before Violet had them completely arranged to her taste, and L'Ombrellino became as comfortable and luxurious a house as it had been when her mother was châtelaine. Especially remarkable was the profusion of flowers inside, bursting from vases, enormous set-pieces, a particularly Edwardian touch so suitable to the character of the house.

With two country houses and a small *pied-à-terre* in Paris, Violet's life began to take on a routine which scarcely changed for the next twenty years. The best times to be in Florence were undoubtedly the late spring, April and May, and autumn, September and October. Then she would return to Paris, spending most weekends in the country, either at St Loup as hostess, or being entertained at a number of other houses. Violet had always enjoyed a *vie de château* and was by now completely integrated into the grandest French society, the *gratin* as it is known, a tiny exclusive circle of super-aristocrats, who are extremely fussy as to whom they will admit to their ranks. Apart from her family connections, Violet was the sort of guest any hostess might relish: however she behaved, she was never dull. She was extremely witty, quick and receptive in conversation and there was more than a touch of eccentricity which made it all the more fascinating.

Violet had long since ceased to turn aside hints that she was the daughter of Edward VII. Indeed, she lent truth to the rumours by appearing at a fancy dress ball dressed as Queen Victoria and, apparently, looking amazingly like her. If people liked to think she had royal blood in her veins, it amused her to let them go on thinking it.

Close friends were less susceptible. Robin McDouall recalls

collecting Violet from Claridges one day to take her to luncheon. They appeared in the foyer at the same moment as the Duke and Duchess of Windsor, also staying at the hotel. A large band of press photographers had gathered. As Robin McDouall led Violet through the throng, she hissed loudly in his ear: 'Do you think they noticed the *resemblance*?' 'Now Violet,' said Robin severely, 'it's no good trying that line with me!'

Violet had become distinctly Edwardian in appearance, perhaps deliberately because the era reminded her of the happiest time of her life. She could have been writing about herself when she said of Madame de Petitpas in *Les Causes perdues*, 'If this aged little girl has the stubborn cult for her childhood, it is because it is the only thing that cannot be taken away from her. She shuts herself up in it more and more.'[3]

Violet's lifestyle had never adapted to modern times: servant problems were not allowed to exist for her, and if she could afford to run two fully-staffed houses, she saw no reason why her friends could not put up a maid and a chauffeur whenever she came to stay. Ever since the days when she was a débutante, and doting parents had bought her and Sonia a Studebaker, Violet had disliked driving, never learning how to do it properly. She had never done her own hair, arranged her clothes or run her houses. When people invited Violet to stay, or when Violet invited herself to stay, she never came alone.

Violet's life settled into the round of routine of visits between France, and Italy, with occasional trips to London. Since the war, visits to England always included seeing Vita Sackville-West with whom her relationship had turned into a loving friendship. Both Nicolsons came to visit St Loup in September 1950 and were enchanted with it, particularly Vita, to whom Violet decided to leave the house in her will, although in the end she did not. Good relations between the three continued when the Nicolsons visited L'Ombrellino in 1951 and the usual rivalry among the Florentine English community revived. Bernard Berenson was particularly anxious to meet the distinguished English visitors, but without their hostess, with whom he had always been on the poorest of terms. Even Mrs Keppel had fallen out with B.B., and if she had failed to maintain good relations, it was predictable that her daughter certainly would not. How satisfying to be given a chance roundly to snub Berenson at last.

A visit made by Vita alone in September 1952 was not such a success. Violet a year later was less prepared to put herself out for her old friend; the usual endless social round had been arranged for Vita to join, but Vita was less willing to fit in. There were one or two amusing evenings – for example, when Violet persuaded Vita to pretend to be the Princess Royal for the benefit of an arrant social snob, who was completely taken in. But it was the last straw when Violet packed Vita and some fellow guests into the car and sent them to Lucca to visit the Marchese Carlo Torrigiani, assuring them they were expected to lunch. Charming and tactful host though he was, the Marchese did not manage to prevent his guests from guessing that their visit was totally unexpected. Either Violet had obviously mistaken the date or exactly what the Marchese's invitation included. The day passed pleasantly enough, but Vita could not forgive Violet this last piece of irresponsibility, for putting her in such an embarrassing position – exactly the sort of social fix that Vita, now so retiring, simply loathed. Making any sort of social effort was now to Vita a waste of time; being forced on someone unknown and, as she though, uninvited and unexpected, was completely unforgivable. The happy friendship cooled afterwards, and although Violet and Vita always kept in touch, now on both sides, barbed remarks were sometimes dropped about the other.

In 1946 Violet had met a new love, Prince Rolphe de Faucigny-Lucinge ('Princey' as he was known to some of her friends) and he became her escort for a few years. Witty, amusing, and excellent company, the prince came from an old French family and was within a year or so the same age as Violet. He liked to tell rather risqué stories and spoke English with an excruciatingly broad Cockney accent. Violet did not mind this as she thought, probably quite correctly, that really grand French people did speak English with a Cockney accent, because they all had Cockney nurses, but she much preferred the prince to show off his beautiful *ancien régime* French.

On one occasion at L'Ombrellino, when the prince came down to lunch, he was asked by Violet her usual question, '*Qu'est-ce que vous avez fait ce matin?*', and replied, 'I 'ave passed a fat morning, Violette – I 'ave 'eld myself in ze salon all ze time.'!

Violet and the prince spent a great deal of time together, in Paris, at St Loup and L'Ombrellino. Initially, marriage was contemplated, perhaps because Violet thought she would like to be a princess, or because she wanted a permanent fixture at her side. Although she cared, she was unable to make up her mind whether to marry him or not, and if she did, on what terms. He tried to reassure her, telling her he thought they could be happy together, and not to look on the black side. He felt sure things would sort themselves out.

Her indecisiveness kept him hanging on a string, and she alternately taxed him with not caring for her and then treated him peremptorily, rather like a social secretary. What began with affection on both sides degenerated into quarrels, usually about money. Violet had never had serious financial worries, and could be very unsympathetic towards people who had. Eventually the tone of their relationship became strained, and by 1950, the Prince was writing to Violet that since she had never been acquainted with people who were poor, she could not understand what it was like. He was undoubtedly in a horrid position, and could not travel or live in the same style as Violet, without her help. Ultimately the gaps in understanding and prolonged absences cooled their friendship, and they parted.

Apart from Rolphe de Faucigny-Lucinge and furnishing L'Ombrellino, there was another novel, *Pirates at Play*, published in 1950. In the same strain as *Hunt the Slipper*, *Pirates at Play* is set in Florence. Despite her threat, 'It will be vitriolic', Violet Trefusis's love for the beautiful city of her second home streams from the pages. She evokes the sounds of Florence, the endless pealing bells ushering in the day.

'Bells filled the air with their bronze clamour; they jostled and contradicted one another in their morning altercation; now and then, a stronger, deeper note, like a fateful stride, broke into their confusion, imposing its rhythm, rebuking the din.

'Somewhere on the banks of the Arno, a donkey brayed with extraordinary insistence; the baker's boy on his morning round, sang a popular refrain with precocious passion. . . .'

The same bells start again at dusk.

'The bells began their evening pounding. As usual the day would be beaten to death.'

By contrast, those parts of the book that take place in England portray a dull, sunless place where it is always raining, and whose inhabitants read only seed catalogues and *The Times*, and talk only to dogs.

This is a book about finding one's heart. Both the heroines mistake their feelings and become engaged to the wrong man for the right reasons. The Italian heroine, Vica, even goes so far as to marry the wrong man, but by doing so places herself securely in a social class from which she can marry her true lover, the debonair (but aging) Gian Galeazzo.

Written with detached cynicism, this is a highly polished book. The characters are well-drawn, the plot meticulously worked out and the dialogue positively sparkles. It is only too obvious that the author has had a great deal of experience of snobbish Florentine society: especially brilliant is the description of the dinner party given by Princess Arrivamale, from the arranging of the *placement* cards on the dining table – 'the part of the evening's ritual she most enjoyed . . . it gave her a delicious sensation of power' – to the actual conversation at the dinner. How often must Violet have sat at such a table! It is a wonderful picture of rich, smart, spiteful and easily-bored people. Violet cannot resist the odd dig at the British colony in Florence, a group with which she was intermittently at loggerheads throughout her life.

There is even a suggestion of Violet herself in one of the characters, racy Aunt Sybil, never married, but no-one is in any doubt at all that she is not a conventionally sweet old maid.

'"Well, she's had as many lovers as anyone in Italy, I should think, though she *did* wait until she was thirty, before she started; she said she was willing to give respectability a chance, but none of the chaps she fancied proposed, so, on her thirtieth birthday, she gave a party in the course of which she announced that she was about to take a lover, so that the members of the family who proposed to cut her should know exactly where they stood. Since then, she has never looked back. Apparently the chaps who did not fancy her as a wife, were dead keen to have her as a mistress. The family were shocked at first, then, they shut their eyes, Aunt Syb gave such amusing dinners, to which people literally fought to be invited. Besides, her lovers were always jolly distinguished – one was a Prime Minister – in the end the family decided it was an honour to be related to Aunt Sybil. Her, what do you call it, celibacy, has become a legend, something rather rare and beautiful, in fact I think we should all disown her if she got married now!"

'Vica gasped, "But she must be quite old!"

'"Quite, round about sixty, I should say. But there's life in the old girl yet. . . ."'

In this book, Violet is again looking at love, especially young love, from a safe distance. Distance has put it all into perspective. The author has become a detached and amused looker-on, an observer from a secure position high up on the hills of the golden city.

The book enjoyed good reviews, of which perhaps the one Violet liked best was written by George D. Painter in *The Listener* in June.

'Her prose is as pure and glittering as an icicle shining in the sun. But it moves in a smoothly hurtling course, with swift lurches and recoveries into slang, internal rhyme, one-word epigrams; so shall I compare the experience of reading it to being driven at 90 m.p.h. over an icefield, by a driver who knows how to skid for fun?'

1950 was a special year: Violet was immensely thrilled by her official recognition as an author, on being awarded the medal the Légion d'honneur. Princess Radziwill gave a party when Violet was officially presented with her medal by her old friend, General Catroux. The award gave her as much pleasure as almost anything ever had before. From then on, she nearly always wore the ribbon of her medal prominently displayed upon her bosom.

Socially, everything was returning to normal after the war. This was the era of vastly expensive costume balls. Susan Mary Alsop remarked sadly to her friend Marietta Tree in a letter in 1951, '. . . the pansies now outnumber the men at all parties. Is this happening everywhere?'[4]

Pansies were hot news, high fashion in France and in Italy. They dominated the costume ball circuit and popped up everywhere. Suddenly it was madly chic to be homosexual.

After years of privation, people wanted to be frivolous and escape into fantasy. This suited Violet completely, and she was in her element. She was always ready to project herself into a new identity, playing her part with great conviction. She made a great hit as Lady Hester Stanhope in 1956 at a ball given by Marie-Laure de Noailles at her house in Place des Etats-Unis, and at yet another ball given by Marie-Laure de Noailles, she appeared as *la veuve du village* (wearing a staggering picture hat), followed by the ghost of the husband she was supposed to have murdered.

Each ball had a theme: Scottish, eighteenth-century Venetian, *fête de village*, characters out of a particular historical period, and so on. They came in droves: Henry VIII with his eight wives ('Eight?' 'No one dares tell him there were only six'), nymphs and shepherdesses by Dior, the latter with diamond crooks from Cartier, bekilted Frenchmen trying to master complicated reels. The rich spent thousands on a costume for one night. They copied family portraits, raided trunks where their ancestors' clothes had been carefully packed away, picked the brains of their dressmakers, their hairdressers and especially those ubiquitous 'pansies', whose essential stock-in-trade was having brilliant ideas about who to go as, and what to wear.

More conventionally, all Paris was *en fête* in the spring of 1957 for the royal visit. The Queen and Duke of Edinburgh were greeted by tumultuous crowds everywhere they went, and a vast reception was given at the Louvre. Naturally Violet, with her real and assumed royal connections, took a keen interest in the visit, and it was rumoured that she was seen giving lessons in the correct way to curtsey at her corner grocer's shop.

The atmosphere of post-war Paris has been brilliantly chronicled both in fiction and in letters by another Englishwoman in voluntary exile: Nancy Mitford. She had come to Paris in September 1945 and eventually found a tiny flat in rue Monsieur ('Mr Street', as she called it). Ten years younger than Violet, they had known each other in England, and met occasionally during the war when Nancy was working at Heywood Hill's bookshop in Curzon Street. When Nancy came to France and began to make a name for herself with the success of *The pursuit of love*, Violet took it upon herself to introduce Nancy to *le tout Paris*. Initially amused, Nancy soon became irritated with Violet who always insisted people fit in with her plans, at whatever inconvenience to themselves. Although the irritation persisted, and there were complete breakdowns of communication from time to time, there was a lighter side to the friendship. Violet, without any help from Nancy, was a character straight out of a novel, and Nancy could not resist using some of her more outrageous traits for the character of Lady Montdore in a novel she was writing at the time – *Love in a cold climate*. Being Nancy, she could not resist embellishing those traits to a gloriously exaggerated degree, but through the very caricature, managed to convey perfectly the essential impact that Violet had on people. Like Lady Montdore, Violet 'automatically filled the foreground'. Love or loathe, or even both consecutively or simultaneously, one could not help being struck by the sheer force of the personality of Lady Montdore who, wherever she was, took the stage. In Violet's case, this was the result of a dazzling, fast-working intellect, allied to complete self-assurance and social ease, and the undeniable fact that she was a 'character' in society. As for Lady Montdore, it was her 'worldly greed and snobbishness, her terrible relentless rudeness [which] had become proverbial, and formed the subject of many a legendary tale' which made people notice her. Neither could ever be overlooked.

Everyone ought to read *Love in a cold climate* at least once; it is one of the funniest books in the language. Lady Montdore is the villain of the piece, but a villain with a pathetic side, especially after her daughter, Polly, marries the repulsive Boy, and the heir to the Montdore millions, Cedric Hampton, comes to take her place. Touching is the transformation which takes place in the tough old battle-axe, the change from Edwardian *grande dame* to 'Thirties' flibbertigibbet. There is the getting into shape, the total starvation cure at a fashionable clinic (from which Lady Montdore is given the sack: 'Just imagine, no dinner, one orange juice at midnight, and woken by the smell of kippers. So naturally, the poor darling

Nancy Mitford

sneaked out and pinched one, and they caught her with it under her dressing-gown'), the newly painted nails, the diamond bees among the girlish curls. Touching, too, is the change in her character. Dependent, devoted, tenderly concerned, her life revolves round Cedric's happiness and comfort. All the mortifications of the flesh she undergoes are for his benefit, to be beautiful and youthful for him. But there is a reassuring return to normal at the end, when Lady Montdore and Polly are reunited, after the birth, and death, of Polly's baby. 'So the poor little baby died. I expect it was just as well, children are such an awful expense, nowadays.'

Nancy once wrote to a friend: 'It is the worst of taking bits of houses, circumstances, and so on, that people then begin to see other resemblances, and yet I don't know how it is to be avoided by somebody who must write about what she knows like me. . . .' Violet would have known exactly what she meant; in her own work she frequently uses houses she has stayed in as settings for her plots, as well as people she has known for her characters. There are several facets of Lady Montdore that bring Violet forcibly to mind. For example, both Violet and Lady Montdore were inclined to become confused by modern slang ('I know people do say he's a daisy'). Confusion over new slang was one of Nancy Mitford's favourite teases.

Like Violet, Lady Montdore could not resist anyone royal (although most of her royal protégés had long since lost their thrones) or anyone powerful, or in high places. 'Power was a positive virtue in her eyes.' By the same token, they shared a complete indifference to anyone in low places, anyone insignificant. They both delighted at times in making people not just shy, and ill-at-ease, but perfectly terrified.

John Julius Norwich recalls vividly a time when he did not know Violet well, and found himself sitting beside her on a sofa. He embarked on a joke, at the end of which Violet merely raised her eyes to the ceiling, leaving him feeling completely crushed!

But the other side of the coin was charm. If someone interested her, the awe-inspiring battle-axe could suddenly turn nice, become excellent company, vivacious and witty. That was why people were drawn to her; they could not resist the exaggerated appeal of her larger-than-life character. There was always something to tell when one returned from a visit to Violet's, something to laugh about. To Nancy Mitford, to whom jokes were an essential part of life, Violet was ultimately irresistible.

Her arrival in Paris coinciding just then with Violet's return after the war, it was not surprising that Nancy should have been affected by the powerful influence of Violet and that she revelled in knowing such a flamboyant individualist. Exaggeration is a Nancy Mitford trait, too: but not personally applied as in Violet's case. Nancy applied it to accounts of incidents and conversations which happened in real life, reported to her friends in letters, meetings and over the telephone.

But eventually the joke began to wear thin, and after Nancy came to know Violet better, she soon became bored by the 'lady-in-waiting' ritual that she had been expected to play. Violet was no respecter of people's privacy. She telephoned on impulse. Even being told point blank that Nancy was working and did not want to be disturbed did not deter her. Nancy Mitford had come to Paris to write and to be near the man she loved. The social round was of secondary importance.

Afterwards, professional rivalry between the two made things more difficult. Violet was very protective about her writing. Nothing had given her as much pleasure as her medal of the Légion d'honneur. She saw herself in the light of a professional *femme de lettres* (indeed, she had this description put after her name in the Paris telephone directory), and it was territory over which Nancy Mitford was trespassing. *The pursuit of love* was a funny book, *Love in a cold climate* even more so. There was no doubt they were better received than any of Violet's books. *The blessing*, which some consider Nancy Mitford's best novel, was perhaps the greatest source of grievance to Violet because it was exactly the sort of book she could have written brilliantly herself. Set for the most part in France, with occasional trips to England, the plot provided precisely the sort of vehicle for contrasting and comparing all things French and English that Violet loved, and at which she excelled (French country life as against English country life; the French way of bringing up children against English nannies: 'Hyde Park every day, Daniel Neal, steam puddings, Irish stew'; the way a French-man makes love compared to an Englishman; social and married life in Paris as against solid respectability at home). Less polished than Violet's comparisons, they were much funnier. Nancy Mitford's characters reveal in conversation their reactions to similar situations in foreign countries. Nanny reacts vigorously against anything French, which is immediately suspect: 'It would never be allowed at home'. The heroine, Grace, on the other hand, is terrifically pro-French, everything French from architecture to food, clothes and her husband, are all quite wonderful, at least at first. When she discovers her husband is being unfaithful in the afternoons ('dreadfully tiresome always going to bed in the afternoon') she thinks that perhaps solid respectable England is not so bad after all.

Grace's introduction to grand French society is an education.

'"There is the old French nobility and that of the Holy Roman Empire (Lorraine, Savoy and so on). These are complicated enough in themselves, but then we have the titles created by Napoleon, at the Restoration, by the July monarchy and Napoleon III. There are the Bourbon bastards and the Bonaparte bastards. I think you have no special place for your big bastards in England?"'

'"I don't think there are any."'

After this, it is perhaps easier to see why Violet Trefusis encouraged the myth that she was the daughter of Edward VII.

As Nancy Mitford's success as a writer grew more assured, relations between the two women cooled. This was aggravated by the publication in 1953 of *Madame de Pompadour* and in 1957 of *Voltaire in Love*. Although Violet could look more or less with equanimity on the publication of books such as *The pursuit of love*, *Love in a cold climate* and *The blessing*, when Nancy Mitford took to serious historical biography, it was something else again. Violet took her own writing career seriously, despite the fact that she was not prepared to devote regular time to it, and this was definitely encroachment. Envy swelled in her heart and by the end of the 1950s, she was running the risk of making herself ridiculous by deprecating Nancy Mitford's achievements, as well as deriding her French, and her accent.

Nancy Mitford unwittingly brought out the worst in Violet. Both immensely talented, they shared an all-embracing love for all things French, but this only enhanced their appreciation of all things English. Both voluntary exiles they could look across to their native country from across the Channel, distance lending perspective to the view.

The difference lay in the fact that Nancy Mitford, coming from a united, but an increasingly less affluent family background, had learned self-discipline and the need to be alone the hard way. To gain her precious independence, she had had to work extremely hard and to a strict routine. It was only after the success of *The pursuit of love* that she made any real money from her writing, but even so, earning her living was a primary concern in her life. Not so Violet, whose turbulent existence had never involved financial worry. Mrs Keppel's investments in Canada, and South Africa, the result of wise advice from Sir Ernest Cassel so many years before, kept her daughter in the style to which she had always been accustomed. As has been put forward, had Violet like Nancy been forced to earn her living by writing, there might have been some really worthwhile books, but Violet lacked that particular impetus, and the self-discipline which Nancy Mitford had had to instil in herself.

Just as Violet resented what she considered to be Nancy's trespasses on her preserves, Nancy resented Violet's only too real invasions into her privacy, the apparent ease with which she wrote her books, and the 'huge capital sum in Canadian dollars' that made it unnecessary for Violet to press her nose to the grindstone. In a letter to a friend, while working on *Voltaire in love*, she wrote: 'Violet telephoned. As she can write books without working, she doesn't understand the necessity, for those less gifted, of doing so'. Throughout the writing of *Madame de Pompadour*, there had been endless telephonic distractions, which were driving its author crazy with annoyance.

But irritated though she was on occasions, Nancy Mitford remained fundamentally fond of her compatriot, and wrote loving dedications in the copies of her books that she gave her. In 1950, in typical Nancy tease, she dedicated her translation of *La Princesse de Clèves* by Madame de Lafayette to 'Darling Violet, who doesn't

know French well enough to read it for herself . . .'. Darling Violet
also received a copy of her biography of Madame de Pompadour
signed by the author, and on Ash Wednesday 1953 Nancy gave
Violet four beautiful leather-bound volumes of *Les tableaux de la
galérie de S.A.R. Monseigneur le Duc D'Orléans* by J. Vatout.
Written on the frontispiece is one dedication: 'Given by the Duc
d'Orléans to E. Holland May 1827'. Underneath is written 'And
given by Nancy Mitford to Violet Trefusis Ash Wednesday 1953'.
Inside the front cover, the books have the Holland House library
plate. Nancy Mitford was not a person who showered extravagant
presents on people, in fact rather the reverse.

Relations began to cool in about 1954: 'Honestly Violet is the
ruin of a small evening. . . . Violet made up her face 10 times at
dinner. I counted.'[5] But Nancy could still shriek at some of Violet's
more outrageous myths. 'Saw Auntie yesterday. . . . As she always
has to go one better she said she once had a burning affair with
Ostrorog and got in the family way. I said goodness Violet, where is
it? She muttered something about a bumpy taxi.'[6]

Auntie Vi or just Auntie was the nickname which Nancy Mitford
and Harold Acton had invented for irrepressible Violet. Harold
Acton lives most of the year round at La Pietra in Florence and was
therefore a neighbour of Violet's when she was at L'Ombrellino.
Although he had always been a devoted admirer and enthusiastic
guest of Mrs Keppel, Violet had had one of her spectacular
disagreements with him. In the small circles in which Nancy
Mitford moved in Paris and Harold Acton in Florence, they were
bound to come into collision with the superforce that was Violet and
she provided them with endless material for jokes. It is not hard to
see why. Endowed with an immense sense of humour where other
people were concerned, Violet could simply not bring the same
sense of humour to bear on herself. She took herself deadly
seriously. To a Nancy Mitford who had been brought up on jokes,
who 'shrieked' at everything, roared with laughter like Linda,
Violet was an endless source of fun, until Nancy became too ill and
too tired to laugh any longer.

Nancy Mitford's letters are full of half-joking, half-exasperated
references to Violet, and Lesley Blanch, who was a friend of them

both, and also lived in Paris, recalls the endless telephone conversations with Nancy who was shrilly repeating Violet's latest remark.

It was Lesley Blanch who was told by Violet that she distinctly remembered being at Buckingham Palace one day as a child, and being allowed to try on the Crown Jewels. When Lesley Blanch, intrigued but disbelieving, said, 'I thought they were kept in the Tower', Violet glibly replied that they had been at the Palace for cleaning! This story appears, a little modified, in *Love in a cold climate* when Cedric and Lady Montdore spend a happy evening dressing up in the Montdore gems ('Pass me the emeralds, would you?').

Violet provided Nancy with some of the material for one of her most memorable characters, and if Violet ever realised she had inspired parts of Lady Montdore, it is unlikely that she would have minded. As Harold Acton says, '. . . most people delight in recognizing themselves in a book: it helps to persuade them that they exist'.[7]

[11]

She withdrew

Violet broke one leg as a young girl practising dance steps to some new records ('from rapture to fracture'); she broke another in 1950 when leaving the ballet. The accident had its funny side, a ringside seat from the Ritz Hotel where she lay recuperating on a smash-and-grab raid taking place at Van Cleefs, the jewellers in Place Vendôme. (Violet in fact slept through the whole incident, though this did not prevent her from enthralling her visitors with reconstructions of the crime, with embellishments). From then onwards, she walked with a stick, and limped slightly.

But neither age nor failing health could alter Violet's appetite for life. She still adored the social round, entertaining and being entertained, meeting new people and seeing her old friends. She might very well tell her hostess how the meal should have been cooked, or how the furniture could be better arranged, but Violet, as the real-life reincarnation of Lady Montdore, was allowed to get away with such unconventionality now. She was a flourishing eccentric and lived up to her reputation, enjoying it to the full. Her mythomania merely increased over the years. Not content with being the illegitimate daughter of Edward VII, she now boasted that she was thirtieth in succession to the British throne!

Violet had always been plagued by insomnia. The characters in her novels are always lying awake in the middle of the night, longing to sleep but never succeeding, hearing the clocks strike the hours as the night slips away, and still the victim cannot sleep. As Violet grew older, her insomnia worsened and in sheer desperation she would try different remedies. Doctors prescribed new drugs which when taken in conjunction with alcohol, could produce peculiar effects. Violet sometimes appeared rather confused.

She was still writing, however, and in 1958 Philippe Jullian's *Dictionnaire du Snobisme* was published with two vignettes by Violet, the first on her old friend, Cecil Beaton, and the second on Italy. Other distinguished contributors to the Dictionary were Nancy Mitford and Marie-Laure de Noailles.

Violet's piece on Italy is in her best strain. She was brilliant when slightly mocking, commenting on the characteristics of the countries she knew best, and she could never resist a dig at people with whom she was not perhaps on the friendliest of terms.

'As to Florence, it prides itself on being the English Aesthete's Mecca. None of them has ever been able to resist its primitives, its precepts or its inspiring hills. All rush there; some settle there. On each flat little hill a tired genius looks down.

'And then in Italy there is happiness, the snobberies of happiness, the happiness of *appearing* to play a part. I will not say that this happiness does not rely on a sort of wary fatalism and good breeding, but everyone makes at least an effort to appear to be happy even when he is not.'[1]

Philippe Jullian was someone Violet had met after her return to Paris at the end of the war. He had many talents: drawing, painting and writing and was considered to be an authority on *fin-de-siècle* art and literature centred on Paris. His best known works are perhaps his biographies of Robert de Montesquiou published in 1967 and Oscar Wilde published in 1968. He also wrote a memoir of Violet, published in 1976. At St Loup, he decorated an indoor garden room with charming Scottish scenes for Violet; he also did the illustrations for *Don't Look Round*. In 1960 they decided to collaborate on a book, *Memoirs of an Armchair*. Philippe did all the drawings.

The book is a fantasy about the (nearly) 200-year life of a beautiful French chair made by Tilliard. The chair is witness to many fascinating historical events both real and imaginary, and the authors are able, through the chair, which has a charmingly unshockable nature, to observe upon the current scene, and the characters involved. In the process, the authors' detailed knowledge of furniture, china and bibelots, not to mention some more colourful historical personages, comes through clearly and is, one

Violet, joke portrait by Derek Hill

feels, typical of both of them. They would never have written a book about a chair mouldering in the front room of a terraced house in Wandsworth. The chair leads as varied a social life as either of its authors enjoyed, and wherever it finds itself, it is greeted with acclaim and shrieks of admiration.

Philippe Jullian's life ended tragically in September 1977. A close friend took his own life and Philippe's house burned down. It was too much. He felt he could not go on.

Despite buying a flat in rue de Cherche-Midi in 1958, with an enormous drawing-room so suitable for the sort of semi-literary gathering Violet enjoyed presiding over, Violet began to spend more and more time in Florence. Here, 'The expatriates were free to wallow in their pet eccentricities and hoist themselves on imaginary pedestals'.[2] There was Sir Osbert Sitwell at Montegufoni, and Harold Acton at La Pietra, the former immersed in his autobiography and the latter in his writing, his antiques and his love of China. Violet had contacts at most of the big houses in Florence, and there was something mysterious and bizarre about Violet that attracted the Florentines. They appreciated some of her more eccentric qualities, apart from the lavish scale on which she entertained, and the luxury and comfort of her house.

It was to Florence that Violet's relations usually came to visit her, her sister Sonia, and various Keppel relations. During the 1960s, her cousin Viscount Bury came to live permanently in Florence with his wife Marina and their son, Rufus. A fine figure of a man, Derek Bury was a favourite guest at L'Ombrellino dinner parties, and as for his wife, she had in her veins Russian blood which made an instant appeal. Her father was an Orloff-Davidoff, a descendant of the one who had been a favourite of Catherine the Great, and nothing could have been more of a recommendation to Violet who had always admired that formidable figure.

Violet was desolated when her cousin died of a heart attack. Lady Bury and Rufus stayed on in Florence and Violet continued to enjoy their company when she was at L'Ombrellino.

Cecilia Keppel, Derek Bury's sister, was another cousin who had first visited L'Ombrellino when she was eighteen, the year after her mother died. Violet was then in her mid-thirties, a glamorous married woman, but she took an interest in her shy cousin. Marriage, Violet told Cecilia, was not the only alternative, and she should make full use of her talents. Discovering that one of Cecilia's talents was drawing, Violet not only arranged, but paid for, a course at an art school in London. Sadly the lessons were never taken as Lady Cecilia contracted a lung infection. Violet also encouraged the young girl to write, and was almost as thrilled as its author when a short story was published.

Cecilia Keppel married David McKenna, son of Reginald and Pamela McKenna, who were two of Mrs George Keppel's oldest friends, and one of their children, Miranda, became a special favourite of Violet. She came to Florence to join her parents who were staying with Violet for Easter, and Violet instantly nicknamed her Gina, after Gina Lollobrigida, whom she did not think Miranda resembled in the least. For some reason, Violet was an admirer of 'La Lollo' but not of 'La Lauren' 'who is like a huge outsize barmaid or *verseuse de bock*, with a voice like a foghorn and spectacular hips. How anyone –? Anyway, I see she is about to become Swiss, which I think is highly suitable.'

In typical Violet fashion, she wove a fantasy in which any man exposed to 'Gina's' charms would be immediately subjugated. One imaginary victim was François Mitterand, an occasional visitor to L'Ombrellino. Miranda recalls an evening when M. Mitterand was there, and Violet called to her after dinner, *'Dansez, Gina, dansez pour nous!'*. Poor Miranda, alone and without music, had to waft around the room, feeling acutely embarrassed!

When Miranda introduced John Villiers, her future husband, to Violet, he was put through a gruelling ordeal to see if he could possibly be good enough for the cherished Miranda. He emerged with flying colours and strangely enough became a loving admirer of Violet. In 1958, he wrote to Violet to ask if they could spend part of their honeymoon at L'Ombrellino. Miranda's parents had spent part of theirs there too, some twenty-four years earlier. She replied, *'Of course* you must spend part of your honeymoon with me, but not, alas! until the beginning of September, as the servants (especially the cook) are not available till then. I'm afraid I can do nothing about this (you see, they are not permanent). I shall be charmed to have you as from September 1st.

'I must quickly warn you that there is a long list of foreign
gentlemen waiting for the first signs of indifference (to you) in Gina,
one being the probable future French Prime Minister, Monsieur
Mitterand, so you had better read the papers attentively, because
Gina may be called upon to Save France, no woman in her senses
has ever resisted A MISSION. Gina d'Arc will be no exception to the
rule.

'Joking apart, I shall greatly look forward to your visit. You
mustn't mind my being there too. I promise I will endeavour to
keep in the background. It is in the best Ombrellino tradition. My
parents were always being asked to stay there by honeymoon
couples.

'Much love, dearest children,
'From Zia Violetta.'

Miranda and John's son, Daniel, in turn became a favourite.
There is a famous Florentine fable about Daniel. In the last stages
of Violet's life, when she could barely eat or walk, she used to lie on
a sofa in the room where meals were eaten, and at each meal, one of
her guests would be selected to sit beside her and entertain her.
Daniel, aged 12, was quite overcome with the responsibility, and
considerably in awe of his very aged and very sick relative. 'Um . . .
aimez-vous Brahms?' he achieved at last. Violet was enchanted.

It was while in Florence in 1960 that Violet met a young
American who was to become an important figure in her life. Violet
had always enjoyed the company of young people, and John Phillips
had many qualities that made an instant appeal. Apart from being
young, he was good-looking and knowledgeable about antique
furniture and paintings. He too appreciated beautiful possessions,
and beautiful surroundings. He had been born in New York City
and had grown up in America, but as soon as he could, he had set off
for Europe.

John, with Frank Ashton-Gwatkin, became Violet's *bâtons de
vieillesse*, the two men in her life on whom she lent, more heavily as
time passed, as age and ill-health took their toll.

Five years older than Violet, Frank was a marvellously sympathetic person who had had a distinguished career in the

diplomatic service. Outwardly the epitome of solid English respectability (he had been educated at Eton and Balliol and his father was a vicar), there were some unconventional areas in his life. He had married a Gaiety Girl, Nancy Violet Butler from Melbourne, Australia, he spoke fluent Japanese, and had written some novels and poems about Japan under the *nom-de-plume* of John Paris. Lady Diana Cooper always says that Violet stole Frank from her, but whether this was so or not, it was certainly true that after meeting Violet, Frank became her devoted admirer, her most loving and ardent friend.

He was the sort of man who liked to be dominated by a strongminded woman. Lady Astor had been a close friend of his at one time. A tinge of masochism coupled with an almost oriental streak of resignation made him the ideal companion for Violet at her most demanding. But he was also extremely erudite, witty and charming, a man who had diplomacy flowing in his veins, and was therefore the ideal person to put next to Queen Helen of Roumania at lunch. Violet used him unmercifully but Frank did not seem to mind.

At the time Violet met John Phillips, he lived in a flat in the famous Florentine palace of the Guicciardini. Violet would call on him there, arriving breathless at the top of the stairs. He would visit her at L'Ombrellino and Robin McDouall recalls an evening soon after Violet met John when she insisted after dinner on rolling back the rugs and dancing. She told Robin that John's profile was like a head on a Sicilian coin, and announced to him that she was madly in love. From then onwards, Violet and John were never apart for more than a few months, and frequently John stayed at the flat above Violet's in rue du Cherche-Midi. For John, whose favourite boyhood book had been *Orlando*, it was more than fantastic to have as his closest companion none other than Princess Sasha. Violet's world, both real and imaginary, appealed immensely to him.

To establish the basis of this last romance, a glance at the letters Violet wrote John Phillips is enough. She almost invariably addressed him as 'Nemours' and signed herself Clèves, one of her favourite fictional characters. But perhaps, initially, she hoped for something less spiritual.

Violet at a Fancy Dress Ball

'When *will* you realise that with me you have to do with a creature all fire and air, and wind and thunder? *Not* a tame, intellectual, pedantic Sorbonne character, like the Duchesse de la Rochefoucauld. To quote Madame de Noailles "*ma cendre sera plus chaude que votre vie*". Why can't you, won't you, strike the right note? . . . I want you to admit that these liaisons *can* and *do* exist? *Especially in Paris!* It has always been so since the eighteenth century. The reason why you cannot admit them is, that in your country, they do *not* exist.'

Nearing 70, Violet had not only to contend with age, but ill-health, and she was only too aware of the ravages these had wrought on her appearance. Frank Ashton-Gwatkin was permitted to see her at her most vulnerable, but for John Phillips the nature of her desired relationship made her keep him at arm's length, unless she felt herself to be on top form.

In the winter of 1961, she was travelling in Spain with Frank Ashton-Gwatkin when she succumbed to a stomach infection. Thoroughly worried, Frank Ashton-Gwatkin removed her to a luxury hotel in Madrid, from where she wrote to John Phillips, 'I am trying to get a seat on the Boeing to Rome on Thursday. If I succeed, and all is well, ring me up at the Hôtel de la Ville, Thursday evening at about 8, but do not come to fetch us. I do not want to see anyone until I have had at least twenty-four hours' rest. I look simply awful, and must go very slowly indeed'.

By early the next year, she was obviously feeling more confident. 'You have the most sluggish, disheartened, dehydrated handwriting of anyone I know! What has gone wrong with you? I would prefer you angry, unreasonable, discontented, not the humble little professor with more or less satisfactory pupils. *Je n'en suis pas là*. I am millions of miles away from Florence! The Dragon and the Glowworm fable?

'This is NOT how I want you. I detest Reason, Resignation, "Rallentando". I am terribly the reverse of you. . . . I hate the idea of your "growing old gracefully". I have more vitamins in my little finger. . . !'

Inevitably it was to remain a relationship that never really matured. Age was only one of the things against them. John Phillips was however exactly the sort of person Violet needed at the time. A sympathetic listener, he took a real interest in her well-being, escorted her to social engagements and generally looked after her. They both adored being at St Loup together and several years before Violet died she gave him the house where he was able to live for six years after her death, haunted he says, by many ghosts.

In 1963, Violet broke her leg yet again. After a particularly grand dinner party at St Loup, she was trying to shut a window, and fell. Numerous painful operations failed to mend the damage. At her age, the treatment and pain were too much and Violet suddenly aged. She needed John and Frank more than ever. They took it in turns to escort her on her travels and keep her happy. They took her to Spain and to Turkey where she was entertained by Ostrorog, he of the bumpy taxi fame so many years before. And whatever Nancy Mitford's doubts, John Phillips recalls the distinctly romantic atmosphere of a long-dead love affair. Frank and John also helped entertain her friends in France and Italy, for she continued to be an indefatigable hostess until the end.

That same year, Violet made her last visit to Scotland. France, Scotland and Spain: these were the countries that had meant most to her. Her love for Scotland was particularly deep, since it was coloured by her love for her mother and her memories of a perfectly happy childhood.

Writing to Frank Ashton-Gwatkin from Dalmeny House, South Queensferry, she said, 'This evening my hostess took me to see an old tower belonging to them, overlooking the sea.

'I was shown letters from Marie Stuart, Catherine de Medici, Charles I's bible, a Florentine incunabula of Homer, most of Beckford's library, letters from Horace Walpole to Madame du Deffand etc. Afterwards we watched seals gambolling in the sea! Gosh! What a country! I become more Scottish every minute . . .'.

On her return to Claridges, she wrote to John Phillips on 25th August:

'My darling Nemours,

'I have just completed my (triumphal) tour of Scotland – one of the most exciting experiences I have ever had in my life, because everywhere I was welcomed, not only as a relation, but as a vedette.

All of which I owe very largely to my darling mother, my husband's
infinitely glamorous family, and a little – to myself. Monsieur X*
would be counted, if anything, as a *'mésalliance'* like when the
Queen Mother wanted to marry a German princeling. The places I
have been I longed to share with you. . . .

'All my love MacClèves'.

As long ago as 1929, Violet had written in *Sortie de secours* 'What
am I waiting for before dying? I have loved much, suffered much,
travelled much. I should die rich with so much love, so much
sorrow, so many countries.'[3]

Now a new type of sorrow began to hit her, the loss of dear
friends. The first of these was Vita Sackville-West in 1962.

Violet had written in a letter to Vita in 1920:

'Man camelo tuti* so superlatively – it seems like an unbroken
sequence – I did as a child – I do still. It seems the one thing that
must last as long as I last – the one indomitable, the one endurable
thing.'

The hot fire of passion, the burning adoration had cooled, but
Violet had not been wrong. Forty-two years later the essence of that
love still remained. It had endured through their separate loves for
other people, their disconnected and quite different lives.

Vita's death must have set Violet's thoughts wandering down a
path they had not taken for a long time. The passionate years of
1918–1920 seemed light years away as Violet thought about Vita,
the person who had meant more to her than anyone else, who had
set her life on the course it was to take. For Vita she had risked
everything and, in a sense, she had lost. She had put herself beyond
the pale in the eyes of the world of her parents, fled to France, and
tried hard to live it down. She had been reasonably successful.
Except to a small number of childhood friends and friends who had
known her since débutante days, such as Sir Osbert Sitwell, the
Vita story was lost in the mists of time. If hints were dropped from
time to time, they were doubtless taken with the large pinch of salt
that most of Violet's stories seemed to demand. Looking at Violet
now, it did not seem credible that she had once been the beloved of

*Edward VII.
*I adore you.

Vita Sackville-West. They had both changed dramatically. Most people simply thought that it was another of Violet's myths and on the publication of *Portrait of a Marriage* in 1973, some of Violet's friends were simply horrified.

Whatever people believed, however, the passionate love affair had happened and although the reality of Vita failed to match her memory, it was an aching sadness to Violet once she had gone. Vita was the gold thread interwoven into the fabric of Violet's life.

Another friend to go, in 1969, was Sir Osbert Sitwell. Violet had alternately infuriated and amused him, but he had remained a staunch friend, knowing all about her past, completely impassive, completely unshockable. Needless to say, as with any of Violet's friendships, there were ups and downs, and occasionally communication ceased altogether, but Violet truly missed her old friend at the crumbling palace. He was a snapped link with her happy childhood.

The older she became, the more protocol and formality were instilled into her entertaining. It might be the end of the Swinging 'Sixties to some, but Violet was regressing more and more into Edwardian hey-days. As the daughter of a King, albeit illegitimate (and Violet by now thoroughly enjoyed the pretence), certain standards must be maintained. At her own parties, she would come into the room last, her guests having already assembled, been given a drink and, it was hoped, waiting agog for their semi-royal hostess. Violet would then make her entrance, heavily made-up, expensively dressed and glittering with enormous jewels, some of them legacies from her mother. Unlike Lady Montdore, she had not had them reset into bees and daisies, but wore them in the original settings and in the same Edwardian profusion as her mother. One hand held her cane, and the other clung to whichever young man was currently in favour. At dinner, Violet presided from the end of the table. Her brilliant, bilingual conversational skill never deserted her, nor her interest in art in all its forms, particularly books, or her curiosity about people or insatiable desire for all the latest scandal. At the end of her life, when Violet could no longer eat the rich food she adored, nor indeed any food at all eventually, she still gave lavish luncheons and dinners, but often she ate little or nothing, and this upset her guests far more than the voracious Violet of before. The glittering spectre at the head of the table was far more distressing.

It seemed that whoever appeared in Florence in the twenty odd years between the deaths of Mrs Keppel and her daughter wrote in his or her diary, or recorded in a letter or memoir, some variety of feud in the Anglo-Florentine stronghold, and these feuds inevitably included Violet. There was constant rivalry among the expatriates. In 1952, when Susan Mary Alsop went, Violet was feuding with Bernard Berenson and Harold Acton. 'The small expatriate colony in Florence is evidently full of malice – like most expatriate colonies,' Mrs Alsop wrote to her friend, Marietta Tree. As for Bernard Berenson, relations between I Tatti where he lived, or perhaps 'held court' would be a more apt description, and L'Ombrellino, had been bad for years. Many people found Berenson ultimately too much, even indefatigable Gertrude Stein wrote in her *Autobiography of Alice B. Toklas*, 'Berenson had a tendency to be supercilious and so everybody let him go on and on'.

John Julius Norwich was a particular favourite of Violet. She had for many years been devoted to his mother, Lady Diana Cooper, and let it be known that she intended to play *tante à l'heritage* to John Julius. With characteristic candour, John Julius decided he had better do something to earn his good fortune, although it was a well known fact that changing her Will was one of Violet's favourite occupations. He began to include visits to Violet in trips to France and Italy, and as she grew older and more unwell, made special visits to see her. One evening, dining *à deux* in Mrs Keppel's bedroom at L'Ombrellino when Violet was so frail that she had hardly been able to hobble to the table set in the window, John Julius had a distinct impression that Violet was about to tell him about Vita. Reticence prevailed, however, and the story was never told.

Philippe Jullian recalled a particularly macabre dinner party to see in the New Year of 1967, a dinner at L'Ombrellino with the stage set for one of their hostess's more poignant appearances. Looking much older than 73, unsteady from the drugs she had been given to overcome her chronic insomnia, Violet hobbled in, supported by

the butler. For the first and only time, her courage and social sense
deserted her as she sat marooned at the head of the table, unable to
eat or talk, whilst her guests struggled to put on an air of festivity.
Suddenly Violet spoke, 'I'm alone, so all alone!' There was a
deathly silence. The guests sat looking at their plates. Fortunately
the imminent collapse of her party revived the wilting hostess and
she called for dancing, which the younger people present managed
to do between courses, not without more than a suggestion of
gritted teeth.

If people wished Violet would give up entertaining, their wishes
were ignored. Planning menus, arranging the *places à table* to
extract the most catalystic quality from each guest, were distractions. In the last five years of her life, every large party Violet gave
was in the nature of a 'last fling', and then there would be another
dinner for fifty or luncheon to celebrate Florence's links with
Edinburgh, complete with the Lord Mayor from that grey Scottish
fastness, and pipers, Violet herself wearing a tartan sash draped
round her neck. No-one could say Violet did things by halves! Her
parties were triumphs of careful planning and generous spending,
wonderful food and drink, beautiful china and glass, the grand and
the eccentric cheek by jowl.

But each splendid occasion was becoming more and more of an
effort, not only for the hostess, but also for the guests. In Paris,
guests came for luncheon nearly every day and sometimes they
wondered if Violet would last until the end of the meal.

Violet spent most of 1970 in Florence, painfully seeing a few old
friends when she felt strong enough. A source of comfort and
support were letters, and none were more cheering than those
written by Madame Gaston Bergery from Paris. An American
married to a Frenchman, Bettina Bergery was a ravishing beauty
described by Violet in *Prelude to Misadventure* as a 'clandestine
genius . . . indecipherable, unintelligible, utterly disconcerting'.
She knew exactly what would amuse Violet, and her letters are
small triumphs of distraction.

'You know if you survive you'll revive, so survive . . . you must
until the properly and triumphantly dramatic moment – which is
just a question of time – and your duty to your legend to wait for.

'. . . Gaston dined *tête-à-tête* with Marie-Laure Xmas night and said she had never been so old friendish and comfortable and nice. New Year's Day I got up for the first time to go to lunch at the d'Harcourts. Geoffrey was there explaining how he and his maid were tied so tightly on Marie Antoinette's chairs, by the young man with the machine gun who robbed Geoffrey's flat, they have Marie Antoinette's initials from the back of the chairs stamped on their backs for life.

'Going to dine with Elsa Schiaparelli . . . Elsa back from the U.S.A. and her triumph in Philadelphia where her old clothes are exposed forever in the Philadelphia Museum – Elsa less pleased by her glory than displeased by being robbed of her jewels and money in the Hôtel St Regis in New York.'[4]

'The only people who haven't flown away are ill with new grippes and getting worse. Don't regret Paris. It's been sinister. You wouldn't have liked it at all, but I hope and suppose in a week or so it will improve, and when it does, so will you – and come back to Cherche Midi before Quatorze Juillet – I must say this town is a void without you – one wouldn't think your little Boldini skeleton would fill it up so much. Perhaps it's all those Lady Teazle curls and regency puns that do the trick.

'We miss your French mind, Scotch heart and Spanish soul.'[5]

'The season wasn't much – started late and ended early – no big balls, few galas . . . opera shut – too many strikes, too much confusion – Violet Palewski's garden party at Le Marais, Marie-Helene de Rothschild's garden party at Ferriers the only two events. Palewski gave a large reception at the Palais Royal you would have gone to – Carmen de Mailly (Stanislas de Rochefoucauld's sister), son's wedding reception at Armonville in the bois was the big turnout of the gratin.'[6]

A stomach infection had taken a grip in the autumn of 1971, and this made it practically impossible for Violet either to eat or to walk. Sleep of course had always been a problem. The drugs she took for her insomnia and her illness, combined with no food, had a horrific effect, and soon reduced their victim to an emaciated wreck. She was receiving blood transfusions almost daily. It was in this state that Violet left her beloved France for the last time on

Christmas Eve 1971 and travelled to L'Ombrellino. The last three months of her life were agonizing. There was not much anyone could do for her except to try to keep her mind off the torturing pain. The old rift with Harold Acton healed as she grew worse, and her other Florentine friends rallied. Her two beaux stayed at her bedside. As the princess she imagined she was, she held a macabre court from her bedroom, decorated by Mrs Keppel so many years before. In spite of her agonizing state, she was artist enough to the end to appreciate the fantastic effect it all made, her last brilliant *mise en scène*.

To distract her, Frank Ashton-Gwatkin helped her with her last novel, *From dusk to dawn*, and in fact finished it for her after her death. The book is about an eccentric marquis with four very strange siblings, one of whom – Lady Aurora – is determined to rule at their ancestral home, Castle Doom, single-handed. Left in charge, she proceeds to sell the family heirlooms in order to buy a racing car. Although the marquis's tastes have previously run to handsome village lads, all ends happily when he marries the only daughter of some rich and vulgar Americans.

Never meant to be anything more than an entertainment, the book is a series of 'in-jokes', jokes Violet had enjoyed all her life, and stories she had always recounted and which her family and friends recognised as having heard many times before. It should not be taken seriously, especially bearing in mind the circumstances in which it was written.

A dear friend, Nancy Pearson, writing to Miranda Villiers on 5th March, described her last week with Violet.

'After your mother left, and her visit gave Violet great pleasure, I went back and stayed for another week. I noticed a difference. Her strength was failing, and she could no longer make that heart-breaking effort of dragging herself into the *salotto*. The pain in her back, due, I believe to bone decalcification, had become intense. But her mind remained perfectly clear. I was reading Crankshaw's biography of Maria Teresa to her, and if when I picked it up I re-read a paragraph that she had heard already, she always pointed this out.'

Violet was literally starving to death, and it was a relief when she died on 1st March 1972. The clamours over her Will, the various legacies she had left, entertained Florentines and Parisians for months afterwards, and one cannot help thinking how much Violet herself would have enjoyed the back-biting and spiteful gossip, the humming telephone lines. Most of her large estate had been distributed entirely according to her wishes and whims. Her family in England felt above all that they had lost a friend, a person in whom the essential warmth of the heart could never be diminished.

Chiquita de Dampierre wrote a delightful word picture for John Phillips, in memory of Violet.

'Curly hair like a hyacinth, a piercing gaze and a roguish smile. Violet . . . with this name so completely inappropriate to her personality, she made her name as a woman of learning and of wit.

'I knew her in her Florentine villa – L'Ombrellino. Upright, her hand leaning on the ivory knob of her stick. That stick, which was her prop, became in her mind an instrument of majesty.

'Thus she possessed the rare and subtle art of being able to transform her weak points into quirks of character.

'Woman of the world by birth, writer by taste, actress by intention, artist by instinct, epigrammist by nature, she added to the brilliant liveliness of her gifts the friendship of the famous of her time.

'Passionate admiration for her mother, Mrs Keppel, is the keystone of her childhood shaped in the surroundings of a privileged society.

'A fervent little girl with an attentive memory and a voracious intelligence, she knew and loved France, loved too its language which she spoke perfectly.

'Violet has unfurled her petals, curved them back, stretched them out, twisted them, unravelled them, stylized them, and under her ascendancy this flower became a different flower, an orchid, not classifiable, specified "Violet Trefusis".'

An elaborate cremation ceremony in Florence, where the front row of the church was reserved for royalty, and to which all the leading Florentine families came, was followed by a memorial service in Paris. Philippe Jullian recorded it as an 'elegant and not unhappy tribute'.

In London, *The Times* carried an obituary the day after her death. Violet Trefusis, it read, had 'inherited her mother's gift for friendship – and her sharp sense of the ridiculous'.

On 7th March, Frank Ashton-Gwatkin's tribute was published. Violet would have enjoyed reading how Jean Cocteau had observed à propos her wonderful French, '*Tu commences où les autres finissent*'. Frank Ashton-Gwatkin wrote about her generosity, and magnanimity and 'uplifting sense of splendour'. This was the 'official version' of Violet's life, the conventional mark of respect.

Much less conventional and to some (for *Portrait of a Marriage* had still to be published) perhaps too revealing was a short, almost abrupt, contribution from Enid Bagnold. It is a relief to read after the fulsome praise which, though true, omitted so much of the essential Violet that it seemed to give the lie to what her life had been.

Enid Bagnold wrote:

'. . . The privilege of being 82 is that you remember people young. I remember Violet (pre Trefusis) young in years but an old spirit: Luxurious, gay, elliptical, witty.

'. . . I used to stay with Violet (Trefusis then) at Blackboys, a manor house she took for a time. I was embedded there in a Vita-Violet row (pre Virginia); and on Violet's side the row was sprinkled with her wit, in those days indulgent. She had an Eastern habit of giving you what you admired. Which is why a jade lion looks at me now. I never knew her except when she was young. She was a great loss to me.'

Most people reading that in 1972 would of course have missed the point, even had they known who Violet Trefusis was. Her books in English had long been out of print and, in any case, they had not enjoyed the same success as her French novels. To most people, Violet's rise to fame took place in 1973 with the publication of *Portrait of a Marriage* by Vita's son, Nigel Nicolson. Apart from the success of the book itself, some of it was serialised in *The Sunday Times* and this gave the story even more publicity. Some people were horrified that a son could expose his mother in this way.

Portrait of a Marriage takes the form of a diary kept by Vita, and a commentary by Nigel Nicolson. Most of Violet's friends and acquaintances found it hard to recognise the breathless, reckless creature that was Violet in the book. From *Portrait of a Marriage* it is possible to see just how much the love affair with Vita changed her, how it planted her feet firmly on the downhill path towards eccentricity, ruthlessness and selfishness. There is a possibility that had Denys Trefusis been a stronger character, had he been able to provide the loving support of a Harold Nicolson, had he been homosexual too and therefore been able to share with her the agony, or had he been able to inspire some kind of passion in Violet's heart, her story might have had a different ending. As it was, disillusion set Violet's life on the path it subsequently took.

From social rebel, determined to expose the hypocritical conventional lives of the world of her parents to embodiment of those simulated virtues: what a strange course her life had taken. The firebrand who had sworn she would show the world what truth and beauty meant had been put out by the cold water of decent commonsense, defeated by conformity. When Vita left Violet, the rebel in Violet died. There has to be someone for whom to set the world on fire; it cannot be done for oneself.

Lady Sackville wrote in her *Book of Reminiscences* in 1922 about her daughter, 'She is a very difficult person to know. To me, who knows her pretty well, she is "a beautiful mask". She has put on a thicker mask since the distressing V. affair.' Violet too put on a thicker mask. From the loss of Vita onwards, it was to be compromise. She would extract the maximum from every person, every situation, live life to the full, but the essential core would never be there. Violet lost confidence in herself both as lover and loved one; she would not risk such enormous investment of emotional capital again. Never would she expose herself again to the chance of another appalling betrayal. There must always be an escape route, and when the fire became too hot, she would take that escape route.

There were compensations in this life of compromise. Her novels had brought her success, especially in France. She had been awarded the medal of the Légion d'honneur and made a Commander of the Italian Order of Merit. She had travelled widely, met thousands of people some of whom were fascinating, lived a life of great luxury, owned two houses of character and charm. She had no strings, no ties, no attachments, except those of her own choosing, so that she could go anywhere at any time with whomever she chose.

But perhaps the greatest compensation of all was the Violet legend, the shield over the private Violet, the Violet whom nobody saw, the disappointed, the unfulfilled, who felt herself unloved. Living the legend of a joke, a larger than life character, she was protected against her private self. In her reputation she found refuge.

The epitaph she finally chose for herself, 'She Withdrew', is most inappropriate for the terrifying old lady of 78 whose ashes lay buried in Florence. Violet had never withdrawn, she was one of life's dancers till dawn, a sticker to the end. Each generation perhaps produces one or two women who entirely represent it, not because they are more beautiful or more talented, but because they are essentially more feminine. Violet in her rose red dress that spring night at Long Barn, 'the purple ripeness of a plum . . . the heart of red wine', Violet rechristened Geranium by Colette: such a flamboyant creature made life richer, more amusing by her presence. *Quand même, elle avait du style. . . .*

Notes and references

1 The pride of her parents

1. G. Cornwallis-West, *Edwardian Hey-Days*.
2. Lady Randolph Churchill, *Reminiscences*.
3. Sonia Keppel, *Edwardian Daughter*.
4. Letter from Lord Grimthorpe to the author, dated 19 June 1979.
5. G. Cornwallis-West, *op. cit.*
6. Violet Trefusis, *Don't Look Round*.
7. Sonia Keppel, *op. cit.*
8. Violet Trefusis, *op. cit.*
9. *Ibid.*
10. *Ibid.*
11. *Ibid.*
12. Sonia Keppel, *op. cit.*
13. Violet Trefusis, *op cit.*
14. *Ibid.*
15. *Ibid.*
16. Sonia Keppel, *op. cit.*

2 A terrible flirt

1. Violet Trefusis, *Don't Look Round*.
2. Nigel Nicolson, *Portrait of a Marriage*.
3. *Ibid.*
4. *Ibid.*
5. Sonia Keppel, *Edwardian Daughter*.
6. Violet Trefusis, *op. cit.*
7. Philippe Jullian and John Phillips, *Violet Trefusis: Life and Letters*. The translation is by Henrietta Sharpe.
8. *Ibid.*
    'On cherchait vainement quelque suite, quelque brin rapporteur dans le labyrinthe inextricable qu'est ta dernière lettre – labyrinthe hélas! où il manque une Ariane pour me remettre le fil conducteur!

*'Aussi au bout d'une courte recherche, je donne ma langue au chat! – il
fait trop chaud pour s'acharner. A moins que tu ne sois devenue subitement
amoureuse de quelque bienheureux mortel, je m'avoue incapable de lire
entre les lignes. Au fait, cela se pourrait.*

*'En relisant attentivement, voilà que tout à coup une espèce d'angoisse
sourde que je ne qualifierais toutefois pas d'appréhension, vient accélérer
la vitesse de mon coeur, vient faire trembler ma main un petit peu en
t'écrivant. . . .*

'C'est palpitant et c'est triste!

*'Pour la première fois tes deux années de plus m'apparaissent bien
réelles, arrogantes, sinistres. . . .*

*'Mais ne vas pas croire que je n'avais pas prévu ce moment: je m'y suis
souvent arrêtée.*

*'Ah, de grâce, dis-moi que je n'ai pas raison, que c'est mon imagination
endiablée qui m'entraine! . . .*

*'Après tout, je ne suis qu'une femme. J'aurais du songer que peut-être à
ton age une liaison masculine devait s'imposer. Je ferai bien de m'en tenir
là. Je sens que je vais dire des inconvenances. Tu ne riras pas, promets que
tu ne riras pas. Il y a longtemps que je ne te demande plus rien, accorde-
moi cela.* It would hurt so. . . .'

9. Violet Trefusis, *op. cit.*
10. Sonia Keppel, *op. cit.*
11. Nigel Nicolson, *op. cit.*
12. *Ibid.*
13. Violet Trefusis, *op. cit.*
14. Nigel Nicolson, *op. cit.*
15. Violet Trefusis, *op. cit.*
16. Sonia Keppel, *op. cit.*
17. Violet Trefusis, *op. cit.*
18. Vita Sackville-West, *Challenge.*
19. Nigel Nicolson, *op. cit.*
20. Nicholas Mosley, *Julian Grenfell,*
21. Lady Cynthia Asquith, *Diaries 1915–1918.*
22. Violet Trefusis, *op. cit.*
23. Nigel Nicolson, *op. cit.*
24. Violet Trefusis, *op. cit.*
25. *Le charme slave – c'est-à-dire ce mélange de brutalité et de câlinerie, ce
goût du mensonge 'artistique', ce prévu dans l'imprévu, ces enfantillages
et ces excès. . . .*

3 A lark with clipped wings

1. Vita Sackville-West, *Challenge.*

2. *Ibid.*
3. Letter from Violet Trefusis to Vita Sackville-West postmarked September 1918.
4. Letter from Violet to Vita dated simply 'Friday night'.
5. Letter from Violet to Vita postmarked 21 March 1919.
6. Letter from Violet to Vita postmarked 24 April 1919.
7. Letter from Violet to Vita headed simply 'Saturday'.
8. *The Times*, 17 June 1919.
9. Nigel Nicolson, *Portrait of a Marriage*.
10. Letter from Violet to Vita dated 23 June 1919.

4 *Prête à faire toutes les folies*

1. Letter from Violet to Vita written from the Golf Hotel, St Jean-de-Luz, dated July 1919.
2. Letter from Violet to Vita, postmarked 19 September 1919.
3. Lady Sackville's diary, 13 February 1920.
4. Vera Brittain, *Testament of Youth*.
5. Letter from Violet to Vita, postmarked 10 March 1920.
6. Letter from Violet to Vita, postmarked 10 April 1920.
7. Letter from Violet to Vita, postmarked 12 April 1920.
8. Letter from Violet to Vita, postmarked 15 April 1920.
9. Letter from Violet to Vita, dated 7 May 1920.
10. Letter from Violet to Vita, postmarked 20 May 1920.
11. Letter from Violet to Vita, dated 29 June 1920.
12. Letter from Violet to Vita, dated 10 July 1920.
13. Letter from Violet to Vita, dated 21 July 1920.
14. Letter from Violet to Vita, dated 17 October 1920.
15. Letter from Violet to Vita, dated 31 October 1920.
16. Letter from Violet to Vita, dated 7 November 1920.
17. Letter from Violet to Vita, dated 17 March 1921.
18. Letter from Violet to Vita, undated.
19. Letter from Violet to Pat Dansey, dated 14 June 1921.
20. Letter from Violet to Pat Dansey, dated July 1921.
21. Letter from Pat Dansey to Vita, dated 1 September 1921.
22. Vita Sackville-West, *Challenge*.

5 *Paris pouvait tout remplacer*

1. From Violet Trefusis's private papers.
2. Violet Trefusis, *Don't Look Round*.

3. Violet Trefusis, *Sortie de Secours*.
4. Michael de Cossart, *Food of Love*.
5. *Ibid*.
6. Letter from Violet to Pat Dansey, dated 11th August 1921.
7. Violet Trefusis, *Don't Look Round*.
8. *Ibid*.
9. *Ibid*.

6 The green flame . . . hidden in the emerald

1. *The Diary of Virginia Woolf*, Volume *11*, *1920–24*, edited by Anne Olivier Bell. Entry for Saturday 5 July 1924.
2. Letter from Virginia Woolf to Vita Sackville-West, dated 13/14 October 1927.
3. Violet Trefusis, *Don't Look Round*.
4. 'Dans chaque être il y a une porte de secours, c'est-à-dire le culte de soi, sous les manifestations multiples, ce qui fait lorsqu'une obsession devient trop violente, on puisse s'évader, disparaître dans un ricanement. L'inconvénient c'est qu'on ne peut pas toujours revenir. . . .'
5. 'Je suis forcée de reconnaître que je ne possède aucune des qualités . . . ou des défauts qui font prospérer l'amour. Le bonheur me vient des choses, non des êtres.'
6. Violet Trefusis, *Don't Look Round*.
7. 'Nous contournons un parc qui recèle dans son sein une vaste demeure en briques rouges qui doit dater de l'époque de la reine Elisabeth et me rappelle tout ce que j'aime de l'Angleterre; son repos, ses bonnes manières, son humeur, ses épiceries où l'on vend du caviar et aussi des souliers à semelles de crêpe, l'architecture Queen Anne, ses oiseaux, ses revenants. . . .
    'J'aime sa vie de campagne avec ses "housemaids" amidonnées et ses sels pour le bain.'
8. 'Les Ecossaises sont les femmes les mieux équilibrées du monde, mais elles vous diront avec une parfaite désinvolture:
    '-Hier soir, au moment de me coucher, j'ai aperçu la tête du chevalier sur la coiffeuse, cela fait la troisième fois depuis deux mois – passez-moi le sel, je vous prie.'
9. 'Je vous aimais trop, vous m'aimiez pas assez. Je ne savais pas "jouer le jeu", elle me l'a appris. Elle m'a enseigné plus de choses en une heure que je n'en ai appris pendant toute ma vie. C'est une regulatrice, une personne pratique et sensuelle, pratique dans la sensualité.'
10. 'Le salon sentait les tartines beurrées, le thé, le parfum timide des jonquilles. Alexa remit du charbon sur le feu et reprit son inspection de la

table à thé. Un étranger, entrant à l'improviste, eût vu là un repas d'enfants; il était à peine croyable qu'une grande personne s'abîmerait l'estomac en mangeant tant de sucreries. Des petits fours d'un rose improbable s'adossaient à des pyramides de choux à la crême; un gâteau au chocolat bavait des confitures. Dans les anfractuosités des rock-cakes brillaient des silices en sucre. Ne parlons ni des pots de confitures, ni du rayon de miel qu'avait fait éclater son corset de bois et qui se répandait en un flot doré.

'Au milieu de cette étincelante compagnie, les éclairs, noirauds et renfrogneés, se serraient les uns contre les autres comme une famille maussade qui n'aurait pas été présentée. . . .'

11. *'Je me sens terriblement terne au milieu de ces personnalités affirmés qui, chacune, a su créer un genre, ce qui ne veut pas dire qu'elles soient particulièrement heureuses, mais, peut-être que le bonheur ne les intéresse pas. . . .'*

7 La tour prends garde

1. Violet Trefusis, *Don't Look Round*.
2. Violet Trefusis, *Sortie de Secours*.
   'Je n'étais malheuresement pas de ces femmes qui remplacent l'amour par des amourettes.'
3. Violet Trefusis, *Don't Look Round*.
4. Diana Mosley, *A Life of Contrasts*.
5. Violet Trefusis, *op. cit.*
6. Violet Trefusis's private papers.
7. Jean Cocteau, *Portraits–Souvenir*.
8. Violet Trefusis, *Prelude to Misadventure*.
9. Violet Trefusis, *Don't Look Round*.
10. *Ibid.*
11. *Ibid.*
12. *Ibid.*

8 The unexploded bomb

1. Letter from Vita to Violet, dated simply 'Friday 1941'.
2. Letter from Vita to Violet, 16 March 1941.
3. Letter from Vita to Violet, 27 January 1941.
4. Letter from Vita to Violet, undated.
5. *'Peu de choses à te dire d'ici. Les Gautiers sont à St Loup que tu*

retrouveras ayant vraiment souffert un minimum. Quant à moi je suis entre Paris Maisons et aussi Le Calliage des Roches ou sont maintenant les deux garçons – tout ceci se passant avec des difficultés de transport presque insupportables – Enfin, soyons patients! Je voudrais tant te revoir mon dieu, j'ai tant de choses à te dire. Il y a une chanson que nous chantions en prison que commençait ainsi: "Quand tu reverras ton village" et je pense souvent que St Loup irait aussi mon village. . . .
    '*Tendrement je t'embrasse darling*
                                                              Antoinette.'

6. James Lees-Milne, *Ancestral Voices*, entry for 9 April 1943.
7. James Lees-Milne, *Prophesying Peace*, entry for 13 February 1944.
8. Violet Trefusis, *Prelude to Misadventure.*
9. Violet Trefusis, *Don't Look Round.*
10. '*Je ne saurais trop insister sur les services rendues à la France par Harold Nicolson, le plus éloquent de ses interprètes qui, de par son tempérament, sa culture et son esprit prime-sautier, est mieux fait que quiconque pour comprendre les français.*'
11. Violet Trefusis, *Don't Look Round.*
12. Vita Sackville-West, *Challenge.*

9 A great lady

1. Violet Trefusis, *Don't Look Round.*
2. From Violet Trefusis's unpublished private papers.
3. Violet Trefusis, *Don't Look Round.*
4. Susan Mary Alsop, *To Marietta From Paris 1945–1960.*
5. Violet Trefusis, *Don't Look Round.*
6. *Ibid.*
7. '*Tout alla bien jusqu'au jour où elle devint sa maîtresse. Désormais elle se sut perdue. Une guerre civile éclata entre ses sens et son cerveau, lui coupant toute retraite, remplaçant ses activités multiples par une préférence hautaine pour le néant.*'
8. Violet Trefusis, *Don't Look Round.*
9. *Ibid.*
10. *The Times*, 15 October 1947.
11. Violet Trefusis, *Don't Look Round.*

10 To darling Violet

1. Anita Leslie, *The Fabulous Leonard Jerome.*
2. Violet Trefusis, *Don't Look Round.*

3. '*Si cette vieille petite fille a le culte obstiné de son enfance, c'est parceque c'est la seule chose qu'on ne peut lui retirer. Elle s'y cantonne de plus en plus.*'
4. Susan Mary Alsop, *To Marietta From Paris 1945–1960*.
5. Harold Acton, *Nancy Mitford: A Memoir*.
6. *Ibid.*
7. Harold Acton, *Memoirs of an Aesthete*.

11   She withdrew

1. '*Quant à Florence, elle peut se vanter d'être la Mecque de l'esthète anglo-saxon. Aucun d'eux n'a jamais su résister ni à ses primitifs, ni à ses préceptes, ni à ses collines inspirées. Tous s'y ruent, quelques-uns s'y fixent. Sur chaque coteau plane un génie fatigué.*
   '*Et puis, en Italie, il y a le bonheur, le snobisme du bonheur, le bonheur de paraître de jouer son personnage. Je ne dirai pas que ce bonheur ne repose pas sur une sorte de fatalisme discret et de bon ton, mais chacun fait au moins un effort pour paraître ce qu'il n'est pas.*'
2. Harold Acton, *Memoirs of an Aesthete*.
3. '*Qu'est-ce que j'attends pour mourir? J'ai beaucoup aimé, beaucoup souffert, beaucoup voyagé. Je mourrais riche de tant d'amour, tant de douleur, tant de pays.*'
4. Letter from Bettina Bergery to Violet, 16 January 1970.
5. Letter from Bettina Bergery to Violet, 4 April 1970.
6. Letter from Bettina Bergery to Violet, 5 June 1970.

Index